Love's Lure:
God's Project People

Other titles by John Ford:

The Answer is the Christ of AD2000
Searching for the Christ of AD2000 in Saint John's Gospel
Seeking the Christ of AD2000 through Saint Francis of Assisi and
Brother Lawrence
Praying in the Mystical Body of the Christ of AD2000
Introducing the Young to the Christ of AD2000
Spiritual Exercises for AD2000
Looking for the Christ of AD 2000 in the Sayings of Jesus of Nazareth

Love's Lure:
God's Project People

A Third Millennium Vision

John Ford

iUniverse, Inc.
Bloomington

Love's Lure: God's Project People
A Third Millennium Vision

iUniverse books may be ordered through booksellers or by contacting:

iUniverse
1663 Liberty Drive
Bloomington, IN 47403
www.iuniverse.com
1-800-Authors (1-800-288-4677)

The books written by John Ford are the product of Christian Publications for the Third Millennium AD (CPTM) in the United Kingdom, the e-mail address of which is: sirjohnford@gmail.com

ISBN: 978-1-4620-2356-1 (sc)
ISBN: 978-1-4620-2357-8 (hc)
ISBN: 978-1-4620-2358-5 (ebk)

Library of Congress Control Number: 2011908513

Printed in the United States of America

iUniverse rev. date: 09/23/2011

Contents

Part 2—Christ's Teaching

Part 3—Conclusion of Book 2

Introduction

Are we on the verge of a new Reformation? What is God saying to us today? These are questions that we Christians need to answer.

The Reformation in Europe followed the Renaissance of learning of the fourteenth century and led to the breakaway from the Church of Rome. The Protestants took their stand on the authority of the Bible and have since divided into numerous sects.

It is odd that the much greater development of human knowledge in the nineteenth and twentieth centuries has not led to a second Reformation among the establishments of Christendom. Knowledge of Truth and Faith should be complementary. Faith takes over where knowledge leaves off. Where knowledge transforms our understanding, Faith needs to be redefined. The two should never conflict.

Two discoveries have transformed our perception of God's creation. The big bang is now seen to be how it all began some fourteen billion years ago. The process of evolution is now seen to reveal how the realm of matter evolved and how our race was gradually created over more than a million years.

Until the nineteenth century the ancient beliefs ruled people's thinking. People believed the myths of Genesis that the first humans were created perfect and through disobedience fell into disharmony with their Creator. Now science has revealed that those myths had no foundation in fact. The evolution of our race has been shown to be a gradual development out of a bestial state, where creatures act by instinct, into a new state of personal being, where individuals can ponder and reflect and exercise free will and Love.

Recent discoveries about our genetic heritage have revealed its influence on our behavior. We have only recently understood that the appearance of the human personality upon the world scene marked the appearance of a new phenomenon, whose behavior is not only influenced by material genes but also by immaterial thought. Ever since people started recording thought and forming a deposit of thought, from which others could profit, that deposit has increasingly influenced them. As communications have improved, its influence has grown. With the advent of the Internet and global access to its pool of knowledge and thought, we are enveloped in collective thought, and cannot escape from it. The "noosphere" of collective thought prophesied by Teilhard de Chardin in the last century has come into being.

At the same time, our knowledge of the past and our ability to study critically the cultures of the past have transformed our knowledge of the Bible and raised many questions about the texts of the four Gospels as they have come down to us.

Despite this upheaval, the establishments of Christendom have remained largely unchanged in their thinking. The Protestants have retained their belief in the sanctity of the Bible and regard it as God's unchanging Word. The traditionalists of the Roman, Anglican, and Orthodox Churches have retained their view that the ultimate authority for interpreting the Truth resides within their church. Neither Protestants nor Catholics appear to have accepted that God's Word is not written but continues to be the resurrected Christ, and that he is tuning his message to the people of today just as Jesus of Nazareth tuned his to the people of the Middle East of his day.

Neither Protestants nor Catholics seem to have noticed that God works from the bottom up and not from the top down. In the realm of matter, mutations in tiny atoms and organisms seem to effect change. In the realm of spirit/personality, the same seems to be true. Change comes about from the bottom through individuals. Just as in biology it takes time before the results of a mutation survive and take over its species, so in theology time is necessary before new ideas can be shown to be valid. As Teresa of Avila pointed out, the resurrected Christ has no faculties on earth, save those of the people in whom he dwells.

After more than fifty years of almost daily meditation on what the Gospels tell us about Jesus and on what some of the greatest saints have also revealed, I have become convinced that Teresa of Avila was right. It now seems clear that the establishments of Christendom have largely lost touch with their followers and also lost their intellectual and moral leadership. I attribute this loss to their desire above all else to conserve the Truth as it has been handed down from the past instead of listening to what God is saying in the present. They failed to seize the opportunities of the bimillennium in the year 2000. They celebrated the occasion by seeking a return to the values and understandings of the Early Church instead of focusing on the implications of the new perspectives of the twenty-first century and God's Word today. Their liturgies continue to pay much attention to the pre-Christian prophets of the Old Testament and focus little on the much more important testimony of the saintly Christians over the past two millennia.

I make no claim to write this book on the basis of my education and theological qualifications. My claim is based on over half a century of almost daily prayer and meditation, much of which is set out in my earlier books. In the face of the attacks now being launched against Christianity, I came to the conclusion that I ought to try to summarize what God is saying to us, the people of the twenty-first century. I make no claim ever to have heard God speak to me in audible words. I have asked for the Grace to understand what he is telling us about himself today. I believe that he must have inspired that request and therefore wants to accede to it, though my Self may stand in his way. Over the years, I have sensed that I was being given insights that did not have their origin in self and that the time had come when I should put my thoughts into writing in the hope of opening up a helpful debate.

I decided that the most effective way of doing this would be to try to imagine what God is saying in bold print and then to set out below in ordinary print my supporting arguments.

When Francis of Assisi was asked by one of his friends what was the source of his authority, he answered that it was the fact that Christ could not find a less worthy instrument at his disposal.

I do not regard myself as worthy even to stand in the shadow of Francis. The thoughts evoked by my meditations on Jesus have been published solely as thoughts to evoke new thinking among my readers. I make no claims about my attempts to interpret what God is saying to us about himself. They are put forward solely to provoke a debate that could, I believe, reinvigorate and galvanize the forces of Christendom.

Prayer to God

Dearest Father in heaven,
Jesus, my indwelling Master and Friend,
Holy Spirit, my inspiring source of Grace and Truth,
Triune God,
Powerhouse of creative Love
And Creator of all that has true being,
Help me to see and to understand
What is your will for me.
Fill me with Grace,
That capacity to love as you love,
So that with increasing intensity,
Out of Love of you,
I reflect back your Love
And become at one with the eternal furnace of your Love,
Reacting in relation to you
As the three persons of your triune personality
React in their relationship with each other.
It surpasses my comprehension
That you can really think of one
So small and insignificant as me
And will that I should of my own free will
Be at one with you.
Yet that is the message of your indwelling Word made Flesh
And the promise of your inspiring Holy Spirit,
In both of whom most surely I can trust.

Prayer to Jesus

Jesus, dearest Master and Friend,
Out of Love you have condescended to dwell in me;
Out of Love you want to take over my personality
And use me as an instrument in your hands
To further God's purposes of Love
And to extend the network of personal relationships of Love
Centered on God,
Which is the state of heaven.
Dearest Master, with gratitude I recognize
That you have already infected me with the Love
That with the Father and the Holy Spirit you are.
With sadness I recognize too
How often I have resisted the embrace of that Love
And allowed my obsession with self and the desires of the body
To resist that infection.
Trusting in the limitless nature of your Love
And the power of the Grace that is yours to give,
May I answer your Love with Love
And out of that Love
Open my entire being to your indwelling presence
And let the Holy Spirit inspire my mind and rule my will.
Dearest Master, this I pray
In the belief that it was for this purpose
That you took on human flesh
And endured the Passion of the Cross.
Knowing that you did all that for me,
I can pray with confidence that in your way
You will grant what I now ask of you.

Book 1

Creation

Chapter 1

The Godhead

Paragraph 1

We are. (As we had not then sent our incarnated Son and Holy Spirit into the world, Abraham could not have conceived of our triune nature. We, therefore, inspired him to think of us as one.)

The *New Jerome Biblical Commentary* indicates that the Genesis account of creation was one among several similar myths current in Mesopotamia in the prehistoric era of the patriarchs. Their origins may date back to beyond 10,000 BC. They all seek to provide some explanation for the creation of the conditions under which the human race then found itself. They tend to attribute those conditions to supernatural beings, gods, over whom people had no control, and who had to be propitiated.

The Bible provides the account of how one man, Abraham, concluded that there was only one God and founded monotheistic Judaism. The Bible traces the development of Judaism to the point where God intervened through the incarnation of his Son, and describes something of the earliest years of the new religion, Christianity, which he founded.

Existing evidence suggests that primordial people believed in supernatural beings and in the existence of some form of supernatural, spiritual existence underlying the material world. It seems reasonable to conclude that it is natural for people to have a belief in some form of god and in spiritual beings.

In a rational world, where science has taught us so much about matter, we are faced with the fact of the big bang and our subsequent creation and development through the process of evolution. Scientists regard the bang as a singularity, behind which the human mind cannot penetrate.

We therefore face three possibilities:

1. the bang was caused by some force, some great first cause, of which science has no knowledge, but which theists call God; or
2. it had no logical cause, and there is no God; or
3. reason cannot determine whether God exists, and perhaps the answer does not matter, as it is irrelevant to our existence.

Cynical Voltaire, for me, hit the nail on the head. He said that God defined would be God finished, and that, if God had not existed, man would have invented him. The creature can hardly define its creator, and anything which the time- and space-bound human reason can define can hardly be infinite and eternal and beyond the singularity of the bang. Any god who could be defined by the human mind must have been invented by it. God has to be accepted not by reason but by faith and assumption #1 is an act of faith.

So, too, is #2. The human mind can no more prove that God does not exist than it can prove that he does exist.

Faced with these two conflicting acts of faith, it is tempting to choose #3 and decide that there is no need to choose #1 or #2, because both are irrelevant to our existence.

The French mystic Pascal suggested that any act of faith was to some extent a wager on the unknown. He argued that a wager on the Christian faith was justified, because the odds were eternity to nothing: if you bet against and lost, you were doomed to eternal separation from God; if you bet against and won, you would gain nothing, since you would soon be dead anyway.

I prefer to look at the effect on human conduct of adopting #1 or #2. There is ample evidence in human history of religion as a force of hatred. Christians have been as guilty of atrocities as adherents of other religions. But there does seem convincing evidence that the force of Love has a benign influence on the human personality, and that a belief in Love/God as the great first cause does exercise a beneficent influence on people. Those who believe in and love the God revealed by the resurrected Christ see this clearly. Those who have no Love in them cannot see it. Looking at the world about me, I prefer to take my cue from those who show Love and, therefore, plump for #1.

Paragraph 2

We are a personal being. We exist in infinity and eternity.

The Israelites seem from the beginning to have thought of God as a personal being. The Genesis myth has God creating man in his image and thus, by implication, regards the human personality as having a divine quality. It is possible that the earliest human thoughts about God arose from people's observation of the element of personality, which distinguished them from other creatures. The human personality seems to transcend matter. It cannot be measured in terms of height, breadth, length, and weight. It is not time- and space-bound in the same way as matter; nor is it really definable. Its qualities suggest that it might belong to another form of being. What we know about animism and the belief in spirits among primordial people indicates that they were very much aware of the forces of nature over which they had no control and saw in them evidence of the existence of an underlying spiritual state of being.

As they saw spirits as neither time- nor space-bound, people thought of them as eternal and infinite. Can we reasonably think of God as other than both?

Paragraph 3

Outside us there is nothing. We are a light shining in darkness. We are the ground of all being. We are the great first cause.

The opposite of "being" must presumably be "not being" (i.e., nothing). John put it beautifully in his gospel. The image of light shining in the dark is so graphic.

By the middle of the first millennium BC, particularly in India and the Far East, people began seriously to study what they considered the spiritual ground of their being and sought to tune their own personality into it. They felt that all the suffering and disharmony in the world must be the result of a breach between matter and spirit, and that a conscious attempt should be made to attain to a state of "at-onement" (meaning a state of being at one with) with the latter. Thus began the movement known as mysticism. Its adherents developed techniques of concentrating on achieving unitary knowledge of the ground of our being. Buddha and his followers achieved notable success, and mysticism, or "The Perennial Philosophy" as Aldous Huxley described it in his brilliant study, has played an inspiring part in the development of Judaism, of Christianity, and of Islam. It cannot reasonably be disregarded as a fact of human experience; nor, as the agnostic Huxley concluded, should the experience of those who have achieved unitary knowledge be ignored as mere self-delusion.

Paragraph 4

Being infinite and eternal, we are beyond the comprehension of your finite and time-bound mind. You must accept that we shall remain a mystery, at least so long as you retain the limitations of your humanity on earth. Nevertheless, the impact of our energy does provide you with insights into the nature of our being.

God created matter to provide the environment under which personalities/souls could be created. He must then have known that by making them time- and space-bound and giving them minds operating with similar restrictions he was cutting them off from direct knowledge of him. I imagine that a reason for this was his desire to give them free will. Had we been born with unitary knowledge of God, we could hardly have achieved it voluntarily and would have been automatons. He did, however, want to give people clues about himself, which they could understand if they so wanted. These clues seem to lie within the impact of his energy.

Paragraph 5

We are three persons in one God: Father, Son, and Holy Spirit. Each of us loves the others, and in pouring out Love on the others, increases his capacity to love. Love is thus created in the furnace of our Love.

For centuries the Israelites held to their belief in God as one in defiance of the convictions of their neighbors and enemies. It had been the rock on which their nation had been founded and on which it had survived. The incarnation of God's Son in the person of Jesus was a break with the past, even though Jesus had, through his ancestry, education, and culture, come out of the past. The earliest Christians were mostly Jews. There is little indication in the New Testament that they saw in the Father, Son, and Holy Spirit the three persons of the triune God. That concept seems only gradually to have come to the fore. The so-called Johannine comma, the expansion of 1 John 5:7–8, by the words "because there are three who testify in heaven, Father, Word and Holy Spirit; and these three are one," does not appear until the end of the fourth century AD.

Nowhere in the Bible do I sense that the writers accepted and understood the dogma of the Trinity. Francis of Assisi gave me my first insight through his understanding of the nature of Love. He saw clearly that Love grows through its outpouring, and that the recipient of an act of Love thus becomes the creditor of the doer, not the debtor. He knew nothing about atomic reaction and could, therefore, not think in terms of chain reactions, as we might do.

Love requires more than one person to be active. A unipersonal God could neither know nor be Love. That God is triune is what makes him Love, and the source and creative furnace of Love.

Paragraph 6

Individually and collectively, we are the force of Love. Where Love is, we are. Wherever Love is not, there is the darkness of nothing, of not being.

That God is the force of Love follows logically from what has gone before. In the dark, light is wherever it is visible. Anything it hits glows with its beams, even if they are reflected. The same appears true of Love. It shines within the human personality. In God it is an aspect of his personality and being. It cannot be separated from him. He is the force that Love is. He is that which makes being being. As Jesus reiterated, he is life. In the realm of the spirit there is no life without him, just as in the dark there is no light, where nothing is touched by light's beams.

Paragraph 7

As the personality of artists is visible in their works, so our triune personality is visible in our creation. As a thought is alive in the mind of the thinker, our creation is alive in us.

Great art holds a mirror up to nature and conveys something of the personality of the artist. This is conveyed through a transfer of feeling, attitude, and emotion. This is particularly so in music. We can recognize the great artist in his work. Great artists seem alive in their works. If that is true of the human personality, must it not be true of God's? I am sure it is. If we look at his creation with Love, we see it shot through with Love, and the tapestry of human history glows with Love's golden threads. It is alive in God. It is alive with God.

Paragraph 8

Is there not something distinct between your mind, your thought, and your will? Yet your actions are the product of all three acting in unison.

This thought came out of a comment on the Trinity in an anonymous book, *We Believe*, published privately in 1983 by a priest. It was obtainable through Dr. Mathias in Peterhouse College Cambridge. The writer thought of the mind conceiving as the Father, the thought conceived as the Son, and the unity of will between them as the Holy Spirit. It is a percipient analysis.

Paragraph 9

Are not the person who commissions and pays for a building, the architect who designs it and supervises the builder, and the builder three separate entities? Yet the creator of the building is none of them acting individually but all three acting together.

This metaphor of the creator of a building is more mundane but seems equally valid. God must be expected to convey his eternal truths through simple metaphors tuned to people's changing circumstances. Jesus's parables indicate how adept he was at so doing.

Paragraph 10

Love grows with its outpouring; and the capacity to love grows with use. Our personalities of Father, Son, and Holy Spirit create Love, spiritual energy, through their reactions to each other.

This is an amplification of the relationship of the three persons of the Trinity in paragraph 5 and leads into the following examples of how God's material creation holds a mirror up to the underlying spiritual reality.

Paragraph 11

Is not the energy of the sun produced through the reaction of its elements to each other?

This is one example of how our physical creation can be seen to mirror, albeit faintly, our underlying spiritual reality.

Another is the way in which the "quantum soup" of matter mirrors the state of heaven. In the former, all the elemental particles are interrelated and held together by the forces that govern the laws of physics. In the latter, all souls are interrelated and held together by the force of Love into a common relationship centered on us.

The church would seem much more relevant to people if Christian liturgies and preachers got away from the language and imagery of the Bible and used those of the third millennium AD. Just as students of art study the personality of artists through their works, theologians should look to God's creation for pointers toward a better understanding of him.

Jesus spoke of the "kingdom of heaven" and used the Judaic imagery of God as a sort of super monarch, because that was the way in which the people and he himself thought. In our day monarchy is mostly discredited as a form of government, and we think more in terms of states. Judging by the way in which our understanding of God's Love has grown over the past two millennia, I think it is more compatible with Jesus's teaching to regard heaven as a state of relationships rather than a hierarchical spiritual court. We are in heaven if we are at one with God in Love.

Paragraph 12

Human marriage at its best reflects that at-onement through Love, which governs the relationship between the three persons in our triune Godhead.

An old definition of "sin" was "missing the target." It is a sad reflection on our age that we concern ourselves so little with the ideal of marriage and concentrate so much on accepting failure and the second or third best. That God is incompatible with sin but loves the sinner gives us good reason to deplore the second best but at the same time to show every sympathy and consideration for those (most of us) who fail to hit the mark.

Traditionally the word "marriage" has been used to describe the union between a woman and a man. Marriages are essential in the creation of families. Families are the building blocks of heaven and the means for the continuation of God's Project People. The word should not be debased by use to cover other forms of civil union.

Paragraph 13

Love is outward-looking. The true lover joys in pleasing the beloved.

The longer I live, the more convinced am I that Grace, the God-given capacity to love as God loves, provides the answer to every moral issue. Without Grace we have no hope of living as God designed us to live. Paul summed it up beautifully in 1 Corinthians 13. Without the outward-looking Love, which is God, we are doomed to become self-centered. We cannot avoid sin by a self-centered act of the will. We can only avoid it when we are so in love with the Love, which is the impact of God on us, that our desire is to please him and to reflect on him and on others the Love that he beams on us. Love displaces sin.

Chapter 2

God's Project People

Paragraph 14

We, Father, Son, and Holy Spirit, experienced such joy in our relationship with each other that we wanted to extend it to beings outside our being and thus both to increase our joy and the capacity of our relationship to create Love.

We therefore entered upon our Project People to create a being in our image (i.e., with a personality with the potential to love as we love and thus to be at one with us in loving).

The traditional and biblical concept has God's act of creation as a fact of the past, and the adventure on which we are now embarked is the human race's redemption from its fall into sin and breach with its Creator. Over the past two hundred years our scientific discoveries and acquired knowledge have conclusively shown that this concept does not fit the facts and must be wrong.

We were not instantaneously created. We are the product of an evolutionary development, which has taken place over millions of years and which is still going on. Physically we have inherited the genes of species out of which we have evolved. Psychically we are influenced by those genes and also by the experiences of our ancestors and by our inherited culture, traditions, and knowledge.

Myths and legends passed on by word of mouth were for centuries the repository of human thought. Only some ten thousand years ago, when literacy and written records began, did people really begin to live under the influence of an independent record of collective thought, but then communications were such that its accessibility and influence were severely limited. Only recently have communications become so effective that both accessibility and influence are rapidly becoming global.

It is now abundantly clear that we are part of an ongoing process of creation and that the history of the human race has to be seen from a different perspective and in a different light.

When he entered upon his project, God must have understood fully its implications and complications and the way in which it would develop. He could not possibly have wanted our race to remain ignorant, as suggested by the Genesis account of the forbidden fruit of the Tree of Knowledge. The whole point of our creation was for us to be at one with him in loving, and thus to share in his knowledge and experience of loving. The story of the human race thus far has been the record of its slow emergence from acting out of bestial instinct into rational behavior and of its increasing ability to ponder, to reflect, and to love.

Paragraph 15

To love as we love, that being, you, had to be endowed with the free will to choose whether to love or not to love. Without that freedom, no one could understand Love or be able to enter our relationship of Love and become at one with us in Love.

That we have to have free will in order to be able to Love seems obvious. An automaton could not love in the true sense of the word. Angels, if one believes in their existence, cannot be conceived of as loving God as humans have the potential to do.

Paragraph 16

We knew that our project would involve much joy and much suffering and that we would share fully in both. We also knew that Love would be much enhanced thereby.

I have heard people rage against God because his project has involved such suffering. I have been tempted to do the same. Because he is all-knowing and eternal, he must have known what would be involved when he entered upon the project and knew what its outcome would be. Christ's Passion (paragraph 42) for me provides the answer. From the beginning God has been personally and intimately involved in that suffering. In the mysterious way in which Love operates, it has thereby been enhanced, and our race as a whole will be shown in the end to have benefited from and shared in that enhancement.

Paragraph 17

The way in which we have created human beings over eons has been the way to create the beings whom we wanted to bring into existence. By evolving people in the way in which we did, it was possible to create a being with a personality in our image and with free will. The element of chance, which was involved in the process and which plays such a part in your life on earth, ensures that you are not a puppet in our hands. Our force of Love drew the process to the point where the soul, the embryo of a human personality in our image, came into being.

If we believe that God is the personal being who is the ground of our being, it seems reasonable to assume that he created the human race in the way in which he did because that was the way to achieve his object. Had any other method been used, it would not have achieved his purpose.

I have assumed that to create a being with free will, God had to introduce a hands-off element in the process, and that that element was chance. At the same time, God had to ensure that the chancy elements in the process of evolution had to be subject to some force to ensure that they produced the end-product, people like us, who were the object of the exercise. I believe that that force was Love. The process was so gradual, and has been so hidden in the mists of the past, that we have no idea exactly how and when the first souls came into being.

Paragraph 18

Love is our energy and is the force that powers you and gives life to your soul/personality. Your soul/personality's life on earth is our

womb, in which it is designed to seek to grow into at-onement with us and thus to prepare itself for eternal life after death.

The newborn baby has characteristics but operates by instinct like an animal until it begins to exercise some thinking control over itself and starts forming a personality. The Grace, or capacity to love, with which the child is endowed at birth, will grow if the child allows Love to direct its will or will diminish if the child becomes increasingly self-centered. As Love is outward-looking, the Love-inspired person will establish a network of loving relationships and grow spiritually in the process. To be self-centered is to be inward-looking. Self-centered people close in upon themselves defensively and diminish spiritually.

The choice before people during their life on earth thus seems to be between spiritual growth and spiritual diminution, between spiritual life and spiritual death, and people's physical death is the moment of truth, when they emerge into their purely spiritual state of being. If, at the time of their death, they have no love in them and no relationships of love with God or anyone else, they may find themselves so alienated from the conditions of afterlife in the overwhelming presence of God that they cannot face it and return to the nothing out of which they were created.

Unlike the fetus in the mother's womb, while their soul/personality is gestating in life on earth, people have the ability and responsibility to think and decide for themselves.

Paragraph 19

Love cannot be taught. It has to be modeled and exampled and assimilated. That is why we made the family the building block of human society. At its best the family mirrors the Love that lies at the heart of our triune nature and that infects people with Love.

The fact that Love has to be assimilated, not taught, strikes me as obvious. Equally obvious seems the fact that potentially the best place for Love's infection to be spread is the family. By thinking and talking of God the Father as Abba (Dad), Jesus indicated the importance of the family as the building block of the state of heaven. It is no accident that atheistic regimes, such as the Communist and Fascist, attack and undermine the family as an institution. Family loves and loyalties are the greatest obstacle to tyrants' ambition to subject people to the state and through the state to themselves. One of the most powerful indictments of the failure of Christian leaders in the democracies of the world lies in their failure to stand up for the family as an institution and to oppose measures (e.g., fiscal discrimination against marriage) that weaken the family as a social institution.

Paragraph 20

Because we made you in our image, your personality reflects ours and has the potential, through the exercise of free will, to achieve at-onement with us in Love.

Among the most worrisome features of modern society in the developed countries seems to me the "depersonalization" in every walk of life. It is visible everywhere, and notably in the medical and legal professions, where personal relationships are not what they were before increasing knowledge and the complexity of modern society forced specialization. Business too is helping the process on through its disregard of the individual and its ruthless subjection of individuals to the short-term demands of the balance sheet.

There is sanctity about the personality/soul of the individual. Individuals, not societies, have been designed to achieve at-onement with God. In the end, individuals will bring society as a whole into at-onement with God (the establishment of heaven on earth). It will be individuals who bring about that day, even if God's project has a collective beginning and end.

Paragraph 21

To begin to understand a personality, you have to love it.

God created the human personality, and he did so out of Love. He understands everyone, because he loves everyone. As Huxley pointed out, the common denominator of all mystics is Love. Only the person who is Love-inspired and adopts Love's way of life can begin to understand what mysticism is about. Self-centered people are so inward-looking and so defensive in attitude that they cannot understand how Love can make another person tick.

Paragraph 22

A personality is like a song. A song has to be heard to stir the heart. If you try to understand it by analyzing its parts, that analysis does not stir your emotions. If you analyze a joke in an attempt to discover why it is funny, the analysis does not make you laugh. To know us, you must be in love with the Love that we are. To know yourself, you must see yourself as we see you.

This strikes me as the sort of language Jesus would use had he lived today.

Paragraph 23

Our Project People is to you an unfinished song. To us it is finished. To us it is like a novel, which we have written, and which we can see as a whole. To you it is an unfinished tale, in which you are the characters. The fact that we know the end does not predestine you.

There lies the mystery of your free will. Your finite and time-bound mind will only see into this enigma when you have shed the limitations of your physical existence. When you see us face to face and see yourself as we see you, you will see the relationship between your time-bound human existence on earth and infinite and eternal existence on the plane of the spirit. The secret lies in the all-encompassing power of our Love.

We have to recognize that God will always remain a mystery to our time- and space-bound mind. In any attempt to help us to peer into the cloud of mystery that surrounds him, God would use metaphors, knowing that they would only help us to see "as through a glass darkly." The parallel of a novel, in which we are the characters, seems to me valid up to a point. Anyone who has written an original story and become wrapped up in it must have experienced the feeling that the characters are taking over. God meant his characters (us) to take over, and he gave them free will, so that they could do so. Because God is Love, Love must be at the center of the mystery he is; only through the unitary knowledge that is given to us through at-onement with him will the secret eventually be revealed.

Paragraph 24

If you examine a tree with a microscope, you will see wonderful detail, but you will be unable to perceive either the tree or the forest of which it is a part.

Physicists, who examine the minutiae of our creation, perceive a "quantum soup" of particles of energy held in a relationship with each other by forces such as gravity and the strong and weak forces. They trace the evolution of matter back to the big bang, which brought it into being. They will be no wiser about the cause of the bang or the reason for the laws of physics.

Likewise, biologists are able to trace the evolution of the human species and to plot the genetic code, which has determined so much of your development. On close examination, the mutations of evolution may appear to them to be the product of chance. Can any theory of probability explain the fine-tuning of the bang? Yet, without that fine-tuning the human race could not have come into being.

If all came into being by chance, how came reason? Who teaches you your appreciation of beauty? The scientist or the artist, poet or composer? From whom do you catch Love? The scientist, the artist, or the person who loves?

The human mind tends to put on blinkers, which restrict its vision and cause it to reach faulty conclusions. This is true of people in every walk of life. Theologians and lawyers seem particularly prone to do so. Christian theologians' blinkers tend to be the Bible and accepted dogma. Jewish theologians are "blinkered" by the Talmud and their Scriptures, and Muslims are by the Koran. Lawyers' blinkers are determined by the US Constitution and body of law under which they are operating.

My warning against putting on the blinkers of biblical thought is not an attack on the Bible. For the earliest Jewish converts to Christianity, the evidence of the Jewish Scriptures and prophets, as interpreted by Jesus and the apostles, was of great importance. After all, they had no other supporting evidence. For us, two millennia later, the evidence of the experience of members of Christ's Mystical Body seems far more important than pre-Christian prophecies of debatable interpretation, important though these are for any understanding of the mind of Jesus of Nazareth. Nevertheless, the good news of the Gospels and New Testament is the best surviving record of Jesus's life on earth and of the earliest days of the Christian church. It provides the basis of our faith and is the essential subject for prayerful meditation. The thoughts distilled in this book would have been impossible without the years of meditation recorded in my earlier books.

God, operating through his creation in action all around us, seems to me to pose the questions in these paragraphs, and the answers point to him.

Paragraph 25

Was not the last phase of evolution the development of a being with mind and will, a person, the development of a new phenomenon? Your human personality obeys neither the laws of physics nor of biology. Being created in our image and being spiritual, you are beyond the measurements of science, applicable to matter. You stem from the ground of all being, the Love, which we are. You obey the laws of Love, or you die.

Not many books have seemed to me mind-blowing. One that "blew my mind" was Teilhard de Chardin's *The Phenomenon of Man*. It had never dawned on me that the human personality could be regarded as a new phenomenon, like, for example, the first mammals, and that its appearance ushered in evolution's acting on a new immaterial plane: the plane of the personality/soul, the plane of the ground of our being.

If God is Love, that plane must be the plane of interpersonal relationships, the plane on which the unifying force is Love.

Chapter 3

The Incarnation of the Son

Paragraph 26

Once we had created people, spiritual beings with free will, one last step was necessary before the purpose of our project could be achieved and human beings could achieve their potential of at-onement with us. Because Love is assimilated and not taught, we had to reveal ourselves and inject our personality into the human race. Only then would people be able to experience what our Love is and learn to love us, as we love them.

This last step was the incarnation of the Son in the person of Jesus of Nazareth.

When God embarked upon his project, he must have envisioned the incarnation of the Son. He could not have expected people to be able to love him unless they could know him. The incarnation was his act of self-revelation in the fullest terms capable of being understood by the human mind, a perfectly lived human life. It was also a recognition that Love has to be caught not taught. By living on earth, the Son would inject his personality into the collective personality of the human race and infect it with his personality, as a gene transfer infects the body and changes it.

Paragraph 27

Over centuries our Holy Spirit had been leading people toward a better understanding of God. By the end of the last century BC, the world was ripe for the incarnation. There were enough Jews alive with the capacity to understand the message of the incarnated Son, the Word made Flesh (as John described him), and communications were such that the message could be spread effectively through the Roman Empire.

The time was ripe. Had the incarnation taken place in the Stone Age in some isolated family or tribal group, it would have been of little effect. The human race had to have advanced into the era of record keeping, and society had to have evolved to the point where news could be effectively and rapidly disseminated. The date of Jesus's birth marked the ideal moment for God to act.

Paragraph 28

To achieve our purpose of revealing God in the highest terms capable of being understood by the human mind, a perfectly lived human life in at-onement with us, the Son voluntarily accepted all the limitations of being human. He became temporarily finite and time-bound. He knew only what the Jews of his time knew about the universe, and the Jewish Scriptures and history provided the basis of his understanding. The culture and traditions under which he grew up shaped his mind, just as they shaped the mind of other Jews.

To live a human life, Jesus had to be fully human. That meant that the Son had to accept all the limitations of time- and space-bound humanity. Like the Jews of his time, he had to have through his mother the genes of his ancestors and a mind shaped by the knowledge, culture, and traditions of the society into which he was born. God had chosen the Jews as the vehicle for his purpose and inspired them to provide the circumstances for the Son's incarnation and birth as a man. At all times up to his death, Jesus operated within the limitations of humanity.

The life of Jesus of Nazareth and the record of what he said and thought have to be viewed in that context. His revelation of God was full and complete within that context. Within their limited perspectives, the people of his day could not take in anything fuller.

The resurrected Christ is in no way bound by those limitations. In him the Son has reverted to his spiritual state as the Second Person of the Triune God. His revelation of himself is limited by the human race's ability to understand. That ability develops as our knowledge and perspectives change. That is why it is so dangerously wrong to regard the Word of God as anything but the resurrected Christ, the resurrected Word made flesh.

Paragraph 29

There is a mystery about this incarnation, and you may well ask how the infinite and eternal Son could become finite and time-bound.

If you think of the circumference of a circle, you can see that it is infinite. So too is the surface of a sphere. On the other hand, a chord joining two points (a and z) on the circumference is finite. In the context of eternity, our Project People is like that chord.

Jesus of Nazareth came out of the past, but his incarnation represented a break with the past. The resurrected Christ, being timeless, is past, present, and future. What matters to you is your relationship with him in the here and now. In the eternity of a heaven, which is unbounded by either time or space, the here and now determines all relationships.

The incarnation is a mystery and is a part of the mystery that God is. The illustration in this paragraph is not an attempt to explain the mystery. I am not a mathematician, and the symbols of higher mathematics mean nothing to me. I have, however, found the image of the chord in a circle helpful.

The Indonesian mystic who drew my attention to the star of light in the tiger's eye jewel in his ring said that the vertical bar of light represented the spiritual plane of our life and the horizontal bar the physical. Where the bars crossed was the bright point of the star and symbolized the all-important here and now. In the relationships of life, the ones that count are in the present. When death brings us face to face with God in the afterlife of the spirit, our reaction is going to depend on our relationship with him at that moment.

In the infinity of eternity, which is beyond the realm of our imagination, a consciousness of being borne on by time seems unlikely. Our relationships with God and other people may share the unchanging quality of the Love that he is.

Paragraph 30

Through his Passion, Jesus showed how we operate. Love creates even out of evil and suffering. We are Love.

This must surely be the lesson of the Passion. See also paragraph 42.

Paragraph 31

From the moment of the Son's resurrection and the coming of the Holy Spirit, the circumstances of our project changed. Previously our process for the generation of personality, with the potential to be at one with ours, had been incomplete. Afterwards it was complete, and people could love what they could know.

In the person of the resurrected Christ, we were on earth, as we had never been before. The resurrected Word made flesh was and still is the Word. He operates, as Jesus of Nazareth did, directly with individuals on the personal level.

Through his death and resurrection, the Son resumed our infinite and eternal nature but has continued a presence on earth in the people in whom he has dwelt and now dwells spiritually, because of their love of the Love, which he is.

More than ever, as a result of his experience as Jesus of Nazareth, he has loved individuals and longed to be loved by them: to absorb their personality and to be absorbed by them; to lead them through at-onement with himself into at-onement with our entire Godhead.

How wise it was to divide the calendar into the eras BC and AD to underline the significance of the incarnation. How important it is to resist the efforts of anti-Christians to substitute BCE (before the common era) and CE (the common era) for BC (before Christ) and AD (year of our Lord). "Common era" is meaningless. AD is a constant reminder that we live in the presence of the resurrected Christ.

The incarnation was indeed a watershed in human history and in the working out of God's project.

As a result of the resurrected Son's experience as a human, God was involved as never before in the human race, and the bond of Love between him and us was stronger than ever.

Paragraph 32

You are the product of the past, just as the fulfillment of our project will be the product of its past. Your part in that fulfillment will not have been forgotten.

Looking at the prodigality of evolution, it is easy to develop doubts about God's Love. How can he have allowed so prodigal a process to come into being? Why should suffering have been involved on such a scale and so apparently pointlessly? What significance can heaven have for people whose circumstances in this life on earth are such that they never have a chance to develop their soul and personality in the way of Love?

My comfort is to trust in God's Love. When his project has achieved its purpose, it will be seen how over its course individuals will have contributed to that end and how their every act of Love strengthened the power of Love and contributed to the working out of God's purpose. Their acts of Love proceeding along the chord of time in the sphere of God's infinity will have made their mark and stand out as points of light.

Paragraph 33

As the butterfly flies from its chrysalis, you are designed eventually to fly free from your body and to achieve at-onement with us, if through Love you so desire.

The metaphor of the butterfly has appealed greatly to me. How can a creature of such beauty and vitality fly so freely out of a chrysalis? May not the transformation of the soul and personality be even more remarkable as it flies into afterlife, free of its body?

Paragraph 34

Does the butterfly worry about the caterpillar out of which it developed or seek to revert to it? No. Nor should you worry about the apparent inconsistency between the profligacy of evolution and our Love.

The analogy is not perfect because the butterfly has no capacity to ponder and reflect. It operates by instinct. God intends us to operate by reason in trust in his Love. That Love provides us with the instinct not to worry, if only we trust in it, accept it, and let it rule our will.

Paragraph 35

In heaven you will share in our joy, the joy of our three persons in their relationship with each other. You will become a part of our furnace of creative Love and add to it. You will radiate Love in harmony with us. As you reflect back the Love of those on earth for you, both you and they will share with us in the enhanced brilliance of our Love.

I regard death as a release from the physical limitations of the body. It seems reasonable to assume that what goes on is the same soul/personality, which has been born into life after death as a spiritual being out of the womb of its physical existence on earth, and which possesses the individuality it acquired on earth. If its relationships of Love were its real life, those seem unlikely to lose their continuity and must be deemed likely to be in effect after death.

Provided that we are willing to be caught up in God's creative furnace of Love, we shall through the power of Love play our part in it. This is a comforting thought, even if the proviso ought to be an alarming reminder of the importance of Grace. Jesus constantly emphasized that we are all children of God. We are all in the family, whether in this life or the next, unless we have, through lack of love, opted out and reverted to the nothing out of which we were created.

Paragraph 36

Our Love and the Love of all at one with us in heaven is unchangingly beamed on you, as we lure you on to accept it and join us there. You will understand that when you see yourself as we see you.

Everything that Jesus is reported to have said, and the evidence of the saints, in whom the resurrected Christ has dwelt down the past two millennia, lead me to believe that God's Love and the Love of all at one with him in heaven are beamed on us.

I suspect that our moment of truth about ourselves will come after death, when we suddenly see ourselves as God sees us (i.e., as we really are). What shock and shame will then be ours, as we see how far short we have fallen of what we were designed to be and could have been! Let us hope and pray that shame will not then drive us from God back to the nothing from which we were created.

Chapter 4

The Mystical Body of the Son

Paragraph 37

On the first Pentecost, as we, speaking through the incarnate Son, had promised, we sent our Holy Spirit to those first believers in the Son. Through our Holy Spirit, we charged them with the power of Love and provided the energy with which they could through the resurrected Son pursue the path of at-onement with us.

An electromagnet does not work unless the power is switched on. The human soul/personality does not work according to design unless Love switches it on. We shall never, in this life at least, know exactly what happened at that Pentecost. Luke's account in Acts 2 was based on hearsay. The historic fact is that something must have happened to turn a band of disillusioned and demoralized friends of Jesus into the resolute group who built up what is now a global Christianity, and did so in the face of all the opposition the Jewish and Roman establishments could muster against them.

The Bible is full of poetic imagery and symbolism, and to this day the people of the Middle East delight in flowery and colorful language. We talk about being "fired" with zeal and enthusiasm. The great mystics talk about the ecstasy of unitary knowledge in terms of fire and light. Luke's "tongues of fire" seems just such language.

Because God is Love, the impact of the Holy Spirit on the soul/ personality is the impact of Love, the implanting of Grace, which transforms it spiritually as radically as a gene transplant may transform the body.

Paragraph 38

We provided the Grace, the capacity of the human will to connect with and be energized by the current of Love.

"Grace" can be understood as the capacity to love as God loves. But to me it is something much more dynamic, which is infused with the Holy Spirit and is the energy of God.

Paragraph 39

We do not force you to love. Individually and collectively we do all we can, while respecting your freedom of will, to cause you to love us. We long for you to want to love us, both as we are in ourselves and as we are in other people. We yearn for your love. We desire passionately to have you at one with us. We want to be indebted to you for the Love that you reflect back to us.

The three persons of the triune God and all beings that have the life, which is God, in them seem to me at one in seeking to lure us of our own free will into that at-onement in Love with God, for which we were created and designed. The fact that the beloved is the creditor of the lover puts God in debt to those who accept his Love; God wants to be indebted to us for the Love that we reflect back to him, both directly and indirectly, through other people.

Paragraph 40

After all, that was why we created you.

We must have constantly in mind the reason why God created us, as explained in paragraph 14.

Paragraph 41

You, the individual, the unique person that you are! What joy it would be for us to have at one with us the unique combination of qualities represented by your personality! You would give us something that no other person could give us. We want you. We need you. We need you to Love us. We most earnestly want you to be at one with us in Love. We long for your Love. The proof of that longing and of our Love for you lies in all the effort that we have put into our creation of you and in all that we did for you in the person of the Son. What Love could compare with that revealed by his acceptance of the limitations of humanity? What suffering he endured for you in his Passion!

God courts us at every moment. Atheists argue that it is intolerably arrogant of people to imagine that the vast panoply of what exists physically was created for our race and is anthropomorphic, particularly when science cannot produce any evidence that it is. I see it as intolerably arrogant of them to disregard the evidence provided by the record of our race's development.

As a theist, I would argue that the fact that God produced that vast framework of creation in order to carry out his project is evidence of the importance that he attaches to us; and that we should face with awe the responsibility that places upon us. All that for me, and I am unique! What a sobering and inspiring thought!

Paragraph 42

To be true to Love and to reveal how we operate, he endured the worst that evil people could do to him. The fruit of his Passion was his resurrection and the birth of his Mystical Body of people in whom he dwells. In that body he has remained present among you. He operates both through its collective personality and through the individuals who comprise it.

Out of the greatest evil mankind could perpetrate, God created for people the greatest good that he could do, in the birth of the Son's Mystical Body. That was the fruit of the Passion. That was the act that revealed conclusively how Love, God, operates.

Paragraph 43

That first Pentecost marked the birth of the Mystical Body of Christ. By absorbing and being absorbed by his personality, people have thereafter been able to achieve that at-onement with us, for which we designed and created you.

It can fairly be argued that Christ's Mystical Body began when the first bonds of Love developed between Jesus and his followers and when they began absorbing his personality and he theirs. But the historic moment must surely have been on that first Pentecost.

Paragraph 44

At-onement with us is a state of being. Heaven is the word that Jesus used to describe that state. Being in it is to enjoy eternal life in the reality of spirit, which underlies the physical existence of human life.

Unfortunately, the imagery of the Bible, which associates God with the pomp of an oriental court and heaven with the splendor of the private imperial garden, tends to distort our vision. Visions of cities paved with gold, where the "saved" will enjoy a life of eternal bliss, are hardly compatible with God's revelation of himself as Love or with Jesus's vision of himself as the suffering servant.

Paragraph 45

In your transitory state of being on earth you are free to grow in Love and be centered on us, as you seek at-onement with us. You are also free to be self-centered and to become increasingly alienated from both us and Love. You will then diminish through spiritual inertia and slip back toward the nothing out of which you were created.

A belief in a hell of everlasting torment is incompatible with a God of Love. What Love or Justice could there be in a system that condemned people to an eternity of hell on the basis of a brief lifetime of a few years on earth? The way in which inertia applies in the physical world seems more indicative of what may happen on the spiritual plane.

Chapter 5

The Growth of Christ's Mystical Body

Paragraph 46

Jesus left no written record of his deeds or messages. He concentrated on teaching a small group of disciples and close friends, who could carry on after his death. This was deliberate. His teaching was personal. The Love that inspired him had to be caught rather than taught. He intended his message to continue to be personal and not to be in the form of some written text, which might be regarded as immutable—a follow-on from the Judaic tradition, which had enslaved the Jews to petty regulation.

This strikes me as obvious. Jesus was evidently literate. Mark 1:21 records him as teaching, and Luke 4:16, records him as reading in a synagogue. Had he wanted to, Jesus could have written down the main themes of his teaching, and something would have been retained at least in people's memory. It has not been. The conclusion must be that Jesus deliberately avoided committing anything to writing. The inference from this must be that he was aware of the danger of written records, having seen how the Jews had been enslaved to their law and tradition. The way in which their lawyers and theologians had interpreted the written legacy of their inspired ancestors was a warning against entrusting his message to writing.

We have only to look around us today at the way in which Jewish, Christian, and Muslim fundamentalists and hate-filled bigots use the

Scriptures to justify their conduct to see how wise Jesus was. Yet the writers of our Christian liturgies increasingly refer to the Scriptures as the "Word of God"! There is only one Word of God. That is the Word made Flesh, the resurrected Christ!

It has been the tradition of the Christian church to regard Jesus's revelation of God as full and complete, as it was a revelation in the terms of a perfectly lived human life, and those were the highest and fullest terms capable of being understood by the human mind. That was true at the time of the revelation.

It was therefore reasonable for the early church and its leaders to regard the evidence and teaching of the apostles as definitive. It became the practice later to regard the understanding of the so-called fathers of the church as also definitive, when endorsed by the councils of the church. Given what we know about the political background to those councils and the part that politics played in their decisions, we must conclude that, like all human institutions, they were both limited in their vision and fallible in their understanding.

Right up to the nineteenth century, Christians believed that the world had been created perfect by God and that the disharmony visible was the result of Adam's disobedience. That had been the watershed in human history. Thereafter, God had been attempting to heal the breach.

The discovery that God had not created the human race in the way described by Genesis but had done so by a slow process of evolution should have been to Christian theologians as mind-blowing as Galileo's discoveries were to the would-be scientists of his day. It pointed to the need for a radical rethinking of God's project, of original sin, of the relationship between God and the human race, of the incarnation of the Son, and of the birth of his Mystical Body.

That birth was the watershed in the development of God's project. The pattern of evolution suggests that the evolutionary process is ongoing and that God is evolving his relationships and communication with people to take account of their changing perceptions and developing capacity to understand. The Mystical Body can now be seen as the perfect way by which God continues his revelation in a manner that no book could emulate.

Paragraph 47

All trace has been lost to you of the earliest written accounts of Jesus's life and sayings. The four Gospels in the Bible drew on sources lost to you. They vary. Each is a portrait of Jesus as seen through the eye of the Evangelist, and the contents have been edited to paint the desired picture. The four portraits convey a likeness of the same individual but differ in detail.

As handed down to you in the Gospels, Jesus's words have been subject to editing, translation, misquotation, and bad copying, and you have no way of determining their verbal accuracy. We wanted you only to be given enough detail to enable you to understand Jesus's revelation of us and to enable you to love us through your Love of the resurrected Son. Our Word is Love not writing.

Do not forget that Jesus of Nazareth and the earliest believers in him were Jews, steeped in the culture and traditions of Judaism. The circumstances under which they had grown up had shaped their minds and formed blinkers, restricting their understanding and vision.

The apostles and earliest Christians believed in a Jewish concept of a Day of Judgment at the end of the world and thought that it was imminent.

It took years before a clear enough concept of Christ's Mystical Body had evolved for Paul to proclaim: "I live; but not I, for Christ lives in me." And it took some three centuries before any understanding of our triune nature was formed and generally accepted.

It took over a millennium before people like Francis of Assisi and Julian of Norwich saw more deeply into the unchanging nature of our Love and dispelled the pre-Christian image of us as a monarch, whose wrath was to be feared and who delighted in flattery. Even now, that image persists in people's minds and in Christian liturgies, which regard the Son's Passion as a sacrifice of atonement on the ancient Jewish model, and which project people's anger with themselves onto us.

It took even more centuries before Teresa of Avila pointed out that the resurrected Son has no eyes and ears and mind through which to operate on earth save those of the people in whom he dwells.

These paragraphs point to some of the signs supporting the view that God is tuning his communication with us to our changing perceptions and capacity to understand, and that our understanding is evolving as our knowledge and social circumstances are evolving.

Even now Christian liturgies have not absorbed Mother Julian's perception that of his nature God cannot forgive. The act of forgiving involves a change of attitude on the part of the one who forgives. God's Love and attitude are unchanging and unconditional. It is we who project our anger with ourselves onto God, when we should repent, forgive ourselves, and accept the Love that God always has on offer. The concept of atonement through punishment and suffering is human not divine. It has been a product of people's imagination and of their social experience.

Paragraph 48

The process of evolution has governed the way in which we created your race. It has not ended. You, and the world in which you exist physically, are still evolving. As your knowledge increases, your perspectives will change. The record of your race's collective thought provides an expanding and ever more influential envelope, within which your thinking has to operate.

When Teilhard wrote about what he called the "noosphere," the envelope of collective thought increasingly influencing human behavior, the arrival of the Internet with its global pool of knowledge and of thought was over time's horizon. Now, in the third millennium AD, it is a fact of life.

It is a sad consequence of Christendom's failure to cut the rope tying it to its pre-Christian Judaic past that its leaders have not grasped the Web's significance. Should they not have welcomed its advent with enthusiasm and be striving to ensure that it is permeated with the collective thinking of the Mystical Body of the resurrected Christ?

Paragraph 49

The resurrected Christ takes account of this and tunes his message to your growing capacity to grasp the Truth. You must keep your ears tuned to what he is saying now and not allow tradition or past understanding to put blinkers on your vision.

The speed with which knowledge is increasing and technology is developing underlines the urgency of God's injunction to us to listen and observe the signs with an open mind.

Paragraph 50

Jesus gave you only two commandments: to love God and to love your neighbor. Both can be summed up in the one word "Love": "Love and do what you will," as Augustine of Hippo said. Let Love be the litmus test of your conduct. "Love" sums up all that we are and all that we want you to be!

The two commandments are so simple and so short. They do not need to be clarified by tomes of theology. At bottom, all we need to follow them is Grace and a Love-inspired will.

Chapter 6

The Future

Paragraph 51

During his life on earth, the Son provided signs to convince people that he was what he claimed to be, but people ignored those signs and rejected him. Down the centuries, we have been continuing to provide signs, and people have continued to ignore them and to reject us.

Two millennia is a long time against the time-scale of recorded history. There is no way now that it can be proved that the many miracles that Jesus performed were actually as recorded. The sketchy account of Jesus's doings in the few weeks before the Ascension is in some ways less convincing to the modern mind than the transformation in the disciples. This is hardly explicable without the resurrection.

The most convincing evidence about God's project is provided by the two millennia in which Christ's Mystical Body has been developing. How odd it is that Christian liturgies pay much attention to the pre-Christian Jewish prophets and poetry of the Bible but almost none to the saintly Christians in whom the resurrected Christ has dwelt and dwells!

Paragraph 52

Who could have imagined that, against all the opposition of the Roman and Jewish establishments, a small band of very ordinary

people would found a religion that within three centuries could command the recognition of the Roman emperor and within two millennia become global?

In all of history has any name been known on the global scale of that of Jesus of Nazareth today?

Has any news ever been proclaimed on the scale on which the good news of the Gospels is now spread throughout the world?

Many Christian saints have provided good evidence of the power of God over individuals who have been open to his Love. The facts referred to in this paragraph are valid signs.

Paragraph 53

The purpose of our creation of the human race was its at-onement with us in Love. Are there not more signs than ever before of the convergence that purpose implies?

Rapid improvement of communications is making the world a smaller place and is bringing people together in a way never seen before. Linguistic barriers are toppling. Already a global language is a reality. Already a global pool of knowledge and of thought is in existence in the shape of the World Wide Web.

Despite local signs to the contrary, the world is becoming a more caring place. When have human rights and respect for the individual previously had such prominence in the international agenda of national states? When before have nations and individuals contributed to fight against suffering on the scale of today?

Every sign of caring is a sign of Love in action, a sign that we are operating through people and that people are operating through us on an ever-increasing scale.

I see ample evidence that the world's inhabitants are converging and doing so at a rapidly increasing pace; and that people generally are becoming more caring. That is a sign that the power of Love is growing, and that the human race is advancing toward the at-onement for which people were designed and created.

Paragraph 54

Those who allow us to effect an act of Love through them make a timeless mark in heaven and help us keep a grip on them. Love-inspired deeds form the steps of the ladder reaching to at-onement with us.

Most of us do not see ourselves as God sees us; nor do we see God's unchanging extension of Love toward us. When, after death, we face the reality of his presence, I suspect that we shall be overwhelmed by the dazzling brightness of his Love. If on earth we have turned a blind eye to Love and become alienated from it, we may then have eyes only for the dark. We may then understand that, as God sees us, we are spiritually dead and in that flash of understanding revert to the nothing from which we were created.

Every Love-inspired act gives God something in us on which to take a grip. Let us hope that at our moment of self-judgment, Grace gives us eyes to see that there is still a trace of Love within us, on which God has firm hold!

Paragraph 55

Your scientists draw graphs to project the future. Why do you not also plot the course of Love and thereby learn how Christ's Mystical Body is evolving and how best to help in its growth?

The increasing speed of the evolution of human knowledge and society should be Love's clarion call to you.

The celebration of the bimillennium in AD 2000 seemed the obvious time for the Christian establishments to concentrate their gaze on the development of Christ's Mystical Body and its experience in its two millennia of existence. I found it baffling that, in gloom over the present state of our human race, they showed no excitement over the prospects for the future but seemed to yearn for a return to what they saw as the more golden days of the Bible and early church. It was no surprise that the evangelical decade of the Anglican Church turned out such a damp squib.

Paragraph 56

If the Passion of the Son was the revelation of how we operate, should you not expect that out of future suffering we should create yet more Love? Have faith in us, for we have faith in you!

All God's messages, by virtue of his nature as Love, must be expected to end on a note of encouragement. He could not have started his project knowing that it would fail. All he wants of us is Faith and Love.

Concluding Prayer

Dearest Father,
I know that you want to flood my mind with your Grace
So that with Love-inspired eyes
I may see through your creation
To the Truth that you are.
Grant me the will to be open to you
And a mind ever receptive to your Truth.

Book 2

Jesus of Nazareth

Introduction

Science has no method of peering behind the singularity of the big bang. Any assumption about its great first cause must be an act of faith. Atheistic scientists restrict their conclusions to the realm of matter and assume that there is no God, because their study of matter provides no evidence that there is. They are not concerned with history and do not see that the facts of history, though distorted and obscured by the passage of time, are as much facts of life as are the facts of matter's creation and evolution. Jesus of Nazareth was a fact of history. The religion that he founded is now global and has more adherents than any other religion. This, I suggest, must be taken into account in any attempt to draw conclusions about life. That is why my attempt to understand God's Project People had to include some study of Jesus, who provides the evidence in support of the view that God exists and is carrying out his Project People.

The first Christians had to view his life and significance in the context of the Jewish Scriptures. Other than the facts of his life, they had no other supporting evidence to go on. To me, after two millennia of experience of the operation of the Mystical Body of the resurrected Christ, the Old Testament, though interesting as evidence of Jesus's cultural background, seems largely irrelevant.

Today the validity of Jesus's claims stands on the experience of Christ's Mystical Body over its two millennia of existence and on the record of the people in whom Christ has dwelt and inspired. We need to listen to them rather than to the pre-Christian prophets of ancient Jewry.

We must also expect that the message of saintly Christians will evolve as we evolve under the influence of increasing education and knowledge. Jesus of Nazareth was notable for the skill with which he tuned his message to the people of his day. We must expect the resurrected Christ to do the same. To see, hear, and understand him, we need to have open minds and to remove the biblical blinkers, which so often limit our vision.

I have tried in this book to provide a portrait of Jesus that may appeal to twenty-first-century people and evoke in them an answering Love. I have assumed that anyone wanting to read it will be familiar with the four Gospels. Rather than quoting verbatim from the Gospels in support of my portrait of Jesus, I have peppered my text with references to the Gospels so that readers can easily look them up, if they so wish, and in the hope that they will be encouraged to go to the source of our information and meditate there.

Prayer

Dearest Father in heaven,
You have given me your Son
and taught me that the way to you
is through him:
by loving him
may I become
at one with you in Love.
Dearest Father,
Grant me the Grace
so to focus on the resurrected Christ
that I see in him
the source of Love and inspiration,
designed for me by you.
May he inspire the vision,
Which I now seek to set down.
May I be so inspired by Love
That my vision is infectious with his Love
and draws others
to you in adoration.

Part 1

Jesus's Life

Chapter 1

Jesus's Conception

Since the time of Moses the prophets of Israel had had intimations that God would eventually send the nation a great leader/messiah. He would usher in the Kingdom of God, in which their nation, as his chosen people, would have their place of honor. Over the centuries a belief had grown up that the prophet Elijah, who was believed not to have died but to have been snatched up to heaven (2 Kings 1–13), would return to announce that glorious destiny.

The four Gospels tell us nothing about Jesus's looks or physical characteristics. We have no idea whether he was tall or short, dark or light, of the color of his eyes, or what his distinctive features were. We can assume that he had a beard and looked like most of the other Palestinian men of his day, but we do not know.

Matthew, the most Jewish in attitude of the four Evangelists, records that Jesus's birth was miraculous in that the baby had been conceived by the operation of the Holy Spirit in Mary, his mother. She was a virgin betrothed to a man called Joseph. As a result of some mystical experience in a dream (Matthew 1:18–22), Joseph had learned about her pregnancy but had nonetheless married Mary and treated Jesus as his son. Mark and John ignore the circumstances of Jesus's birth. Only Luke goes into more detail. If, as some tradition holds, Mark was the boy who fled naked from the Garden of Gethsemane at the time of Jesus's arrest (Mark 14:52), Luke was the only Evangelist not to have known Jesus personally and to have relied solely on the evidence of hearsay. Yet Luke is the one to provide all the colorful detail, which goes into the traditional Christmas story. Luke alone tells us the strange story of the conception of John the Baptist, which seems to recall the way in which Sarah, Abraham's wife, had conceived in old age, and provided support for the credibility of Mary's experience. Luke's account, written decades after the event and based on hearsay, is easily regarded by skeptics as the stuff of legend and discounted as such.

The legends of Greece, Rome, and the Far East provide ample evidence of nowadays unbelievable miraculous relationships between gods and people. It is not surprising that people refuse to accept that God could have acted thus arbitrarily in breaking the rules of his creation. Our scientific knowledge does not accept that a woman could conceive a child without male fertilization of an egg. Among living organisms only a few of the more primitive seem able to procreate through parturition without fertilization, though a crayfish has recently been discovered that is able to clone itself. There is, however, no suggestion that Mary cloned Jesus. Given what I understand to have been the Father's aim in the incarnation of his Son, the way in which he brought it about seems logical.

Much of what our scientific and technological age deems as natural would even a few centuries ago have been regarded as miraculous, and it is true to say that the more we know the more we realize there is to know. The human mind is largely a closed book to scientists. If we want to understand the human personality, we look to artists, not to scientists, to enlighten us. Really to understand children or adults we need to love them.

Centuries before Jesus of Nazareth, the peoples of the Far East had come to accept that underlying the physical plane of our life there is a spiritual plane, governed by a spiritual force, which is the ground of our being. Led by Buddha, they sought through religion and the practicing of mysticism to achieve some form of union with that force.

For centuries the Jews had seen in that force the personal God of Abraham and had, like many people of other religions, endowed it with the personal qualities that they saw in the human personality. They envisioned their God as a superhuman king and endowed him with the qualities of the tyrant kings of their experience. Gradually, as the Old Testament records, the Jews modified and softened those views and began to equate him more with Love than power.

To the loveless doubter, the biblical account of the conception of Jesus is meaningless and unbelievable legend. To those who believe in the Christians' God of Love and try to put themselves in God's position, it is not only believable but logical. If God's Project People is indeed to create people in his image (i.e., with a personality capable of achieving union with him in Love), how could they love him without knowing him; and how could they know him, if he was by timeless and spaceless nature beyond their comprehension? It was logical for God to decide that the only answer was to reveal himself through the incarnation of a part of his triune personality, his Son, as we know him. He could reveal God in the fullest terms capable of being understood by the human mind, a perfectly lived human life. He would both love and be loved. He would inject God's personality into the collective personality of the human race. He would change the human race as an implanted gene changes a living organism. He would bring about in people a spiritual mutation, which would enable God's Project People to be successfully completed.

Most of the apostles and disciples, who knew Jesus personally, were probably dead by the time Luke wrote his Gospel. They must have heard of Mary's account of his birth and many must have heard the stories on which Luke based his Gospel. They would no doubt have protested had they radically disagreed with the facts as presented by Matthew and Luke, and the fourth Gospel, written later, would have corrected them, if necessary.

As Shakespeare wrote in *Hamlet*, "there are more things in heaven and on earth than are dreamt of in our philosophy." We cannot exclude the possibility of miracles. If the context of signs of God's power fit into the context of his Project People and our concept of God, it seems rational to accept them at face value. That is why I have accepted as fact that Jesus was conceived by the Holy Spirit and was thus both human and divine.

By human I mean that by accepting humanity through his incarnation, the Son accepted all the limitations of that humanity. He was bound by time and space and limited in his knowledge by the human knowledge of his day. He knew nothing, for example, of modern medicine, evolution, or genetics. His concepts of the world about him were those of the Jewish Scriptures and law, and culture and tradition.

In his divinity he was at one with the God from whom he came. That meant that throughout his life on earth he was always in cahoots with God with a will perfectly attuned to God's.

Chapter 2

Jesus's Birth

One of the great strengths of the Christian religion is that it was founded on historic fact. Jesus of Nazareth was a person, who actually lived. The historians Tacitus (*Annals* 15, 44) and Josephus (*Antiquities of the Jews* 18, 3) mention his death. The four Evangelists record the main events of his ministry but are notably vague about dates and places. Luke dates his birth during the time of the census, when Quirinus was governor of Syria during the reign of Augustus in Rome. Even this is vague, since a census in those days took years to complete. The consensus of scholars seems to be that Jesus was probably born in 7 or 6 BC and certainly before the death of Herod the Great in 4 BC.

Only Luke (chapter 2) reports the circumstances of Jesus's birth. Under the terms of the census people had to go to the place of their tribal origin. This for Joseph was Bethlehem. The town was, therefore, crowded with visitors when Joseph and Mary got there, and all the accommodation was full. While they were there, Mary went into labor. A compassionate innkeeper let her go into his stable. There she had her baby, and, for want of anywhere else, they wrapped him in swaddling clothes and laid him on hay in a manger. Luke may well have included these details to emphasize the lowliness of Jesus's birth.

Luke goes on to say that, in accordance with custom, the boy was circumcised eight days afterwards and later was taken to the temple in Jerusalem to be consecrated to God as a first-born child. There a man called Simeon foretold his future greatness and the anguish that he would cause his mother (Luke 2:25–32). These events have the ring of truth about them and fit in with our knowledge of the customs of the day.

Luke also reports that after Jesus's birth, some shepherds in fields nearby had some mystical experience telling them about the birth and went to the stable to see the baby and to worship him (Luke 2:8–14).

Only Matthew reports that sometime after those event three stately men, perhaps astrologers who watched the stars to foretell events, arrived unexpectedly in Jerusalem from the East (Arabia?). They asked where they could find the newborn king of the Jews. King Herod heard about this with some concern, since it suggested that there might be some threat to his family's hold on power. He summoned the Jewish leaders and asked for an explanation. They referred him to a prophecy that a future leader of the people would come out of Bethlehem. Determined to destroy the baby before he could become a threat to his monarchy, Herod asked the men to report back to him when they had found the baby. Guided by a star (even though Bethlehem was not far from Jerusalem) the three strangers found Jesus and gave him presents of gold, frankincense, and myrrh. After some mystic experience warning them not to go back to Jerusalem, they avoided Herod and went straight home. When he heard this, Herod was furious and had all the children in Bethlehem aged two or under killed (Matthew 2:2–18). In the meantime Joseph and Mary had likewise been warned of the danger and had fled to Egypt with the child.

When reading these accounts set down years after the events, it is difficult to distinguish fact from legend. The same applies, for example, to "The *Little Flowers* of Saint Francis." Even though these were written within a few years of Francis's death, the facts of his life were embroidered and became legend. Both the Gospels and the *Little Flowers* seem to me to be legendary with a purpose: to symbolize the truth and to draw lessons from it.

Thus the early church saw in the gifts of gold and frankincense and myrrh not only typical examples of the wealth of Arabia but also prophetic symbols of Jesus's greatness, divinity, and future Passion.

The slaughter of the Holy Innocents must have been such a traumatic event that it must have figured in the folklore of Bethlehem and of the earliest Christians and have been based on fact. Now, two millennia after the events, it is impossible for us to recover what actually happened. All we can do is to absorb the message that the Evangelists were trying to convey and not to bother too much about the brushstrokes in their portrait of Jesus. That, I am sure, is what we are meant to do. Too detailed a scholarly study of the Gospels can easily become as foolish as trying to study a forest with a microscope.

Chapter 3

The Years of Preparation

The four Gospels tell us virtually nothing about Jesus's boyhood. Only Matthew tells the story of the family's flight into Egypt (Matthew 2:13–15) and their stay there until after the death of Herod the Great in the early part of 4 BC. It is not clear how long the family stayed in Bethlehem before the visit of the wise men. It could have been some months or even a year or more, since Herod had all the toddlers in Bethlehem killed who were aged two or under.

During the time of his stay in Egypt, Joseph presumably maintained the family by practicing his trade of carpentry. By the time they got back to Nazareth, Jesus must have been two or three years old. We hear nothing more of him until Luke's story of him at the age of twelve (Luke 2:41–50). Then, on one of the family's visits to Jerusalem for the Passover feast, he was so preoccupied with talking and listening to the Jewish theologians in the temple that he lost track of time for three days, until his mother caught up with him.

If we really want to love the resurrected Christ so that by loving him we may come to love God the Father, we need to use our imagination to visualize what he must have been like both as a child prodigy and as an adult. I find that the only way to do that is to look about and see him in other people. Like him, other children come out of their mothers' womb with characteristics but only the seed of their personality/soul. Throughout their gestation in their mother's womb they are passively developing physically with no will of their own. At birth their will germinates and their personality/soul comes into being. As they exercise their will and are conditioned by their parents for acceptance in society, their personality grows. As they go through life, the way in which they exercise their will affects the development of their personality.

Luke mentions that Elizabeth, the mother of John the Baptist, was a cousin of Jesus's mother; and that her husband, Zechariah, was a priest, who at times had to be on duty in the temple. It thus seems reasonable to assume that on their visits to Jerusalem, Joseph and family stayed with the Baptist's family. John and Jesus were the same age and must have played together and later shared thoughts and hopes. Jesus would also have absorbed from Zechariah much theology and temple gossip and gotten used to chatting with theologians who visited the house. These visits must have been a joy to the precocious Jesus after the intellectual dullness of the society of Nazareth. They also gave him a chance to hone his intellect against the best brains of his day.

We know nothing about Jesus's life in Nazareth during those formative years. Looking at children around us we can imagine something of what he must have been like. He would have been cheerful and gregarious, physically attractive and a good sport, but also reflective and thoughtful and apt to retire into himself. He was probably popular and a good leader, but his outstanding abilities may have caused resentment in others. Only a few of the children would have been taught to read and write. At the rabbi's school the boys learned by rote, and the rabbis beat the Scriptures into them. Jesus must have learned quickly, avoided the beatings, and perhaps aroused the hostility of other pupils as a teacher's pet. He would certainly on occasions have experienced the cruelty of boys and noted the effects of others' selfishness and malice. Because his father was an artisan and not a landless laborer, he may well have been envied as well as admired for his physical qualities.

In those days, as nowadays in many countries, the family was an extended feature of society. Uncles and aunts lived in close contact with each other, and the children played together like brothers and sisters. Mark talks about Jesus's relations and brothers and sisters (Mark 2:21, 31 and 6:3), and Matthew mentions them too (Matthew 12:46–50), but tradition holds that Jesus was Mary's only child. It is therefore possible that the references were to cousins, members of the extended family. In the early church a book of James (regarded as apocryphal) suggested that Joseph was an old man by the time he married Mary. Joseph might thus have had another family by a first, deceased wife, whose children had already established their own homes and were Jesus's stepbrothers and stepsisters. Whatever the actual situation, it need not affect the image of Jesus in our mind's eye as visualized on the basis of tradition, the New Testament, and our experience of life.

It would have been normal in those days for the son of an artisan to be trained by his father to step into his business. From the time he could walk, Jesus must have been in and out of his father's workshop and been conditioned to lend a helping hand when he could.

The Gospels do not mention Joseph after his return from Egypt. We can only assume that he must have died, perhaps when Jesus was a teenager, and that Jesus carried on his trade in order to provide for himself and his widowed mother. As the business prospered, he may have hired an assistant to free him to spend time with the theologians in Jerusalem and sects such as the Essenes.

There is no indication when Mary or Joseph told Jesus about the circumstances of his conception. I imagine that at first they kept them secret to avoid ridicule and gossip in Nazareth.

Jesus's growing personality and brains must have caused tensions in the family as he developed intellectually and soon surpassed his parents in thought and learning. By the time he was seven or eight he may have been wondering how it was that he seemed abler than all the older people and children of his acquaintance. As soon as his parents could trust him to keep the secret, they may well have told the boy the circumstances of his conception. That would explain the remark to his mother, when scolded by her in the temple (Luke 2:50), that he had to be about his Father's business.

None of the Gospels tell us anything more about Jesus until some twenty years later when he emerged to begin his ministry. We thus have to use our imagination to fill in any detail. In this process, Love is all-important.

If we truly love babies and toddlers just because they are babies and toddlers, we can see in them something of the personality of Jesus when he was a baby and a toddler. The same experience applies in our view of boys and girls, adolescents, and young people. It is said of Francis of

Assisi that he began his sermons by addressing his audience as "good people," because he was always looking at the good in them. We likewise need to look at the people about us with Love-inspired eyes so that we focus on the Christ in them. In this way the resurrected Christ of the twenty-first century AD will become a reality for us.

Chapter 4

The Start of Jesus's Ministry

Given the vagueness of the Gospels about dates, scholars are unable with any confidence to set a date on the start of Jesus's public life. John the Baptist had become a well-known figure. He preached the need of repentance to prepare for the coming of the promised messiah. People had flocked to hear him and to be baptized by him in the River Jordan. He had annoyed Herod Antipas, the ruler of the Galilee district, by criticizing him for having married his brother's wife, Herodias, and was soon to be imprisoned and later beheaded (Mark 6:17–29). Jesus must have been in his early or mid-thirties when the time seemed ripe for him to begin his public life and to pick up the Baptist's call for repentance.

Having waited so long to receive the vocation for which he had prepared, Jesus must have been excited and relieved to receive a clear call. His first action was to visit John and to insist on being baptized by him (John 1:29–34). He wanted his being washed in the river to set the seal on the new public life that lay ahead. All four Evangelists report this incident and the selection of the twelve apostles. John makes no mention of the temptations, which preceded the latter.

Having decided to start on a public ministry, Jesus had to decide how he was going to conduct it. He did as he always did when facing difficult decisions: he withdrew into some quiet and lonely place, where he could lay his problem out in communion with the Father.

As Jesus was alone, when he faced his temptations, he must have told the twelve about them. We do not know how he told them. He was faced with a decision on how he was going to shape his public teaching. What exactly was his policy to be? It would have been difficult at the outset of his ministry to talk to people in the terms of a potentially great leader deciding on his campaign policy, but they would have understood at once the thoughts of a starving man seeking ways to influence people. Hunger must have been obsessing his body in the wilderness as he communed with the Father. The common people were used to being hungry. What better way to gain their support than to use his miraculous powers to feed them? The people wanted sensation. To use his power on stunts would also win him adherents. World leaders adopted the ways of power politics. Why should he not do the same? As he laid these alternatives out in communion with the Father he saw that they were all temptations to distract him from the only course of action that would be compatible with his integrity and with his relationship with the Father. He saw clearly that the only course really open to him was the way of Love. God was Love. His relationship with the Father was a relationship of Love, in which the personality of each was united in Love with the other. He could only extend that relationship to other people by infecting them with the Love that motivated and powered him.

Another question that faced him was how to spread his message. Should he write it down, so that it could be circulated and form a lasting record, or should he leave nothing in writing and rely on his followers to follow in his footsteps and pass on his message by infecting others with the Love that they were to catch from him? None of the Evangelists mentions this decision, yet at some time Jesus must have taken it. He was a brilliant scholar and could quote effectively from the Scriptures in argument. He must have known well how to read and probably also to write, unless he had decided deliberately not to learn how to write. He must have been tempted to leave a written legacy. Yet he could see the dangers of putting words in writing. The Jewish establishment had abused the Scriptures to fasten bonds of petty regulation round the populace and in the process had lost sight of the spirit which underlay them. Written records could always become corrupted through being misunderstood, mistranslated, inaccurately copied, or deliberately falsified or misinterpreted. They could also be regarded as immutable, even when they were no longer reconcilable with new knowledge and were out of tune with the times. His decision must have been deliberate: he would not write. He would rely on personal relationships. He would train his apostles to infect others with the Love with which he was going to infect them. The infection would thus be carried on through future generation of leaders inspired by him.

The selection and training of the twelve thus assumed a task of the greatest importance to the success of his mission. Records do not tell us much about them or exactly when they were chosen. John 1:35–51 indicates that some of them were disciples of John the Baptist. They were evidently simple people of great potential. Jesus called Simon Peter (Rocky), because he saw that he would be rocklike in the firmness of his loyalty. James and John were nicknamed sons of thunder (i.e., in our terms perhaps angry young men). Judas Iscariot proved a traitor, but the rest remained loyal, and, in the end, many were martyred. With the selection of this team, Jesus had completed the launching of his ministry and determined its shape.

Chapter 5

The Structure of Jesus's Ministry

Because each of the Evangelists was, in his Gospel, painting a portrait of Jesus and not writing a history, he did not think of a biography of Jesus based on actual dates and places. Matthew, in his record of the Sermon on the Mount (chapters 5–7), seems to have written a summary of Jesus's teaching, as if to provide a context for the rest of his Gospel. John seems to have used his long discourses to do the same (chapters 5–7 and 14–17).

After years of meditation on the Gospels, I sense that the two years or so of Jesus's public life can reasonably be divided into three periods after its inauguration. The first was the period up to the experience of his transfiguration, recorded by all the synoptic Gospels. During this, Jesus started preaching his message of Love and experienced gathering opposition from people, who saw in it a threat to their interests. The second period was that between the transfiguration and his Passion, during which he was preparing for his suffering and death. The third was the time of his Passion. Looking at Jesus two millennia after these events, we have also to consider a fourth period: the centuries after his death, during which the resurrected Christ has been acting through people inspired by him and the Holy Spirit.

The history of Jesus during the first period is difficult to untangle from the Gospels. John the Baptist probably preached during the years AD 27–29, and Jesus's crucifixion may have been two years or so later after a ministry lasting about two years. Mark sets the start of it in the Galilee region. There Jesus seems rapidly to have impressed people by his teaching and healing touch. Mark reports that only then did Jesus complete the selection of his apostles (Mark 3:13–19). Luke indicates that the success of his healing caused a sensation and forced him to rethink his priorities (Luke 4:42–44). Was he to devote all his effort to healing people or should he give priority to his preaching and teaching? As he was used to doing, when important decisions had to be made, he withdrew into a quiet place and reflected on the question in communion with the Father and decided that his priority should be teaching. To concentrate on miracles of healing, however much they were inspired by Love, could be to fall into the second temptation. So he left the area for a while.

John reports that Jesus went to Jerusalem and carried out his first cleansing of the temple. The other Evangelists only report one such incident and set it during his last visit to Jerusalem during the days before his arrest. That seems much the most logical time for Jesus to have committed an act calculated to infuriate the establishment, and John's first mention may possibly be an error in the text. The other Evangelists merely reported that Jesus left Galilee for Judaea. John reports (chapter 4) that on his way back to Galilee, Jesus passed through Samaria and much impressed the people. John also reports later visits to Jerusalem, when Jesus healed a man at the pool of Bethesda (chapter 5) and escaped stoning by an angry crowd (John 10:31–34, 39). Back in Galilee, Jesus seems to have traveled the area extensively and spent time in the lakeside towns of Tiberias and Capernaum. Mark tells that Jesus even went as far as Tyre (Mark 8:34). Sometimes he stayed with friends or sympathizers, but at other times, as he indicated (Luke 9:58), he and his friends must have lived like homeless tramps. During these wanderings Jesus noted that hostility toward him was increasing.

Hate is the opposite of Love. It was natural that, as Love of Jesus grew among people who admired him, enmity against him increased among people who had little Love in them and felt threatened by his teaching. As he became increasingly aware of this, Jesus must have wondered what his fate was to be. Was he to die naturally like Moses, to be snatched up to heaven like Elijah, or to be killed by the Jewish establishment, as so many prophets had been in the past?

As he did when faced with other dilemmas, Jesus withdrew to lay the issue before God in quiet communion with the Father. On this occasion he took with him his three closest friends, Peter, James, and John. It is strange that John did not mention the transfiguration in his Gospel; nor did he mention Jesus's last agony of indecision in the Garden of Gethsemane, when Jesus chose the same three to share in what was his last temptation. Perhaps these omissions were because the stories had already been widely disseminated and did not easily fit into the scheme of his Gospel. The other Evangelists told the story of the transfiguration (Mark 9:2–13) from the observers' point of view rather than from Jesus's.

Yet, it was Jesus's experience. The clue to an understanding of it lies with the way in which the synoptic Gospels associate it with Jesus's prophecies about his coming suffering and death. The first two prophecies they place on either side of the transfiguration. The presence of Moses and Elijah in the vision indicates that both prophets' experience was very much in Jesus's mind as he faced growing hostility, particularly among members of the establishment in Jerusalem. The three apostles may have been telepathically aware of this; more likely in conversation, Jesus may well have wondered what his fate was to be. It is also possible that Jesus was so aware of the realm of afterlife that he was also in communion with those prophets, seeking guidance from their experience. (It is a comforting thought to believe that Jesus actually did that in a moment of trial, and that we can do the same with saints, whose experience seems particularly significant to us.)

However Jesus reached the answer, it evidently pointed clearly to the answer, death: he was going to be killed by his enemies. Jesus must have understood at once that it would do his cause no good if he was to be assassinated in some dark alley and his body was to be hidden. If he was to be killed, let it be in public in full view at a time when the maximum effect would be achieved. What better time than at the Passover, when Jerusalem would be packed with visiting Jews, including many from abroad. Jesus would not have been human had the thought of his murder not haunted the rest of his public ministry. He would not have been the farsighted person he was had he not planned for it, as events were later to reveal.

In the meantime, Jesus seems to have carried on his ministry as he did before, wandering around Galilee and Judaea, preaching and performing acts of healing. These seem best considered as aspects of his teaching and revelation of God through him. Any attempt to treat them as events, dated and placed in a historic biography, would seem a hopeless task because of our lack of factual evidence; moreover, Jesus wants us to catch from him his Love of God and people and, in reflecting that back, experience the spiritual ground of our being, which lies in the nature of our Creator.

Chapter 6

Jesus's Passion

In the eyes of Jesus's apostles and their earliest Jewish converts, Jesus's death was much more than the sad end of a historic figure. They saw in it the explanation of his life on earth and the culmination of his revelation of God. Being Jews, they saw in it also the fulfillment of ancient prophecies about the coming of a messiah, a suffering servant (Isaiah 53), the supreme sacrifice to atone for sin, and a full revelation of God's Love in action. Jesus himself certainly saw in his Passion the consequences of his integrity to himself and to the way of Love. In his at-onement with the Father, he had no other choice. The Father was not asking for his death as a grisly sacrifice in the spirit of Jewish tradition and law (Leviticus) to atone for human sin. The Father was suffering, as Jesus was to suffer, as a consequence of that sin.

Having decided that the next Passover feast in Jerusalem was the best time from God's point of view for his enemies to wreak their hatred on him, Jesus openly confronted them and brought their hostility to a head. He manipulated events so that his opponents acted of their own free will in a manner best suited to God's purposes. Their judicial murder of the Son was to prove self-defeating and a triumph for God and for Jesus himself.

Jesus's first action was to perform his most sensational miracle, the raising of Lazarus in Bethany after four days in the tomb (John 11:17–53). On receiving Lazarus's sisters' call for help, Jesus deliberately delayed coming to Bethany until days after Lazarus's death, because he wanted to perform a miracle, which would be bound by its magnitude to create a sensation and frighten his enemies. It did. Faced with his probable arrival in Jerusalem for the Passover holiday, the leaders of the Jewish establishment were greatly alarmed, feared the effect that he would have on the crowds in the city, and turned their thoughts to getting rid of him.

Jesus's next action was even more worrisome to them. His triumphal ride into Jerusalem (Luke 19:28–38) was planned in secret, but his friends must have tipped off the people and worked to get their sympathizers out on the streets in a mass demonstration of support. To add to the effrontery of his action, Jesus rode into the city on a donkey in fulfillment of an ancient prophecy about a future king of Israel.

Having thus, as it were, waved a red rag at the establishment, Jesus then went out of his way to antagonize it (Mark 11:15–19). He went into the temple, denounced its desecration by the scandalous activities going on inside its precincts with the connivance of the authorities, and by sheer force of personality created mayhem in its public market. He then went about speaking in the most vituperative language about the authorities (Matthew 23), calling them hypocrites, the epitome of lawlessness, and the successors of those who had in the past murdered prophets; by implication he challenged the authorities to murder him too (Matthew 23:32).

No wonder that his enemies decided on his death (John 11:45–54).

No wonder too that Judas's disillusionment was aggravated by these developments. Like some of the other apostles, he had been chosen for his discontent with the situation in the country and for his potential. Unlike the other apostles, however, he seems never to have surrendered to Jesus in Love but to have persisted in trying to fit Jesus into the image in his mind of the leader whom he felt was necessary and wanted to follow. As Jesus steadily pursued his way of Love, Judas's disillusionment grew. Jesus's confrontational tactics in Jerusalem must have worried Judas even more: they were alienating potential supporters in a nationalist revolt against Roman rule. It was at this time that his alienation from Jesus reached the point where he made contact with the leaders of the priests (Matthew 26:14–16) with a view to working with them against Jesus. The increasingly desperate priests must have been thankful to have a traitor among Jesus's closest friends.

As the main day of the Passover feast approached, Jesus planned events carefully. He was determined to have a last meal with his apostles before his enemies got hold of him. He also wanted his fate settled before the feast, so that he would be the talk of the town during the public holiday. He was adept at seeing through people and by that time must have been aware of Judas's state of mind. He ensured that the arrangements for the Last Supper were kept secret and seemingly only at the meal revealed that he was planning to spend the night afterwards in the Garden of Gethsemane, a location that would appear suspicious to his enemies and strike them as a good assembly point for an insurrection and as a good place to arrest him away from his supporters in the city.

The timings suggested by the four Gospel accounts of these events neither agree with each other nor sound convincing. It is hard to believe that Jesus was arrested after nightfall on that Thursday evening, and that in the ensuing twelve hours or so there was time for him to be brought before and tried by the Sanhedrin, to be taken before Pilate for a preliminary hearing, to be sent to Herod's lodging and to be heard by him, and, finally, to be taken back to Pilate and flogged before Pilate's final sentence. It seems more likely that the Last Supper was more of a farewell meal held earlier than a formal Passover meal. Jesus might, however, have followed a practice of the Essene sect and celebrated the Passover a few days earlier than other Jews.

The normal procedure at a Passover meal was for it to start with the drinking of a cup of wine. This was followed by the filling of a second cup of wine, the drinking of which followed the recounting of the first Passover (Exodus 12). The food was then eaten. Finally a last cup of wine was drunk.

Only Luke and John (Luke 22:24–27 and John 13:2–20) mention that, as they were waiting for the supper to begin, the apostles began arguing about who would have preference in the kingdom of heaven. This prompted Jesus to wash their feet as a lesson in humility and to emphasize that to be true to him they had to serve out of Love and not expect to be served. Peter at first protested over letting his Master perform that menial task. Judas must have regarded it as the clinching evidence that he could not base his hopes on Jesus. He had found out where the party was going that evening. He left the table, while they were still eating, and went out into the night (both literally and metaphorically) to pass on that intelligence.

The atmosphere around the table must have been tense with conflicting emotions. The apostles must have sensed that Jesus was under great strain but not understood the reasons for it. Jesus was deeply grieved by Judas's final decision to betray him and was full of apprehension about what the future held for him. There is no account of the conversation during supper, but all three synoptic Gospels report that, as Jesus handed out the bread and wine, he instituted the Eucharist, which became the central Christian rite. He told them that the bread, which he was handing out, was his body, about to be broken, and the wine was his blood, about to be shed for the remission of sins and a new covenant between God and people, and he instructed them to reenact this in memory of him (Luke 22:14–20). John omits mention of the institution of the Eucharist but summarizes (John 14–17) Jesus's final discourses and teaching. Parts of this may indeed reflect memories of that last evening together (e.g., on the way to the Garden of Gethsemane Jesus may have drawn the apostles' attention to a vine overhanging a wall and used it as a peg on which to hang his metaphor about being the true vine [John 15:1–6]). As a whole, however, these chapters of his record of events seem not so much a record of Jesus's actual words as the product of later reflection on John's memory of them.

When they got to the Garden, Jesus was assailed by fearful thoughts about what would soon be happening to him. He withdrew, taking with him Peter, James, and John, and wrestled with his fears in communion with the Father.

There is no record of what those thoughts were. He had probably witnessed an execution, or at least heard graphic accounts of one. He would not have been human had he not quailed at the thought of undergoing such torture. He had persuaded the apostles and many other people to put their trust in him and make sacrifices in following him. Was he to cause them grievous disillusionment? And what about his mother? Could he really force her to suffer the horror and grief that she would feel over his execution as a common criminal? As he laid these thoughts before his Father he saw ever more clearly that his personal integrity, his relationship with the Father, and his chosen way of Love all demanded his sticking to his previous decision. Three times he put the question to his Father, and each time he sensed the same answer. If Mark was indeed the boy who fled naked from the garden after Jesus's arrest (Mark 14:32–42), he was the person who witnessed Jesus's agony of prayer, as he fought against this last temptation to escape, while the three apostles slept.

Having got him in their power, the Jewish leaders wanted to get rid of him quickly. They wanted his death to appear legal. The alternatives were to convict him of a religious crime, which they could punish by having him stoned, or to convict him of a secular capital offense, for which the Roman authorities would have to punish him. The latter appeared the best course of action, since blame for Jesus's death would then lie with Pilate, the Roman governor. Once the posse had been sent off to arrest Jesus, the chief priest's office must have alerted both the Sanhedrin and Pilate to the danger of an insurrection over the Passover holiday and to the arrest of Jesus as leader of the conspiracy. They probably also emphasized the need for quick action before the day of the Passover feast in order to nip rebellion in the bud before the mass of the population could be persuaded to join in.

Jesus was quickly brought before the Sanhedrin. The trial was summary (Mark 14:53–65). Correct court procedures were ignored. Jesus said that he had nothing to hide. He had spoken openly, and there were plenty of witnesses to what he had said. One of the guards slapped his face for insolence to the court. False witnesses were produced to distort what Jesus had said, but their evidence was inconsistent and unconvincing. Jesus answered none of the charges. Finally the chief priest adjured him to answer whether he was the Christ, the Son of God. Jesus answered that he was. This was hailed as proof of his blasphemy, and the court promptly convicted him. Instead of having him at once stoned for that religious offense, the court remanded him for trial by Pilate.

The priests knew that Pilate scorned their religion and would care little about blasphemy. Pilate found their country difficult to rule, and the Romans were on the watch for treason against Rome. The chief priest emphasized that Jesus was claiming to be king of the Jews and thus was challenging the Roman emperor's rule. Apparently (Matthew 24:19) Pilate's wife had had a dream about Jesus and warned Pilate to have nothing to do with his case. (Perhaps one of her Jewish servants had told her about Jesus and described what a wonderful man he was.) Pilate must, therefore, have been relieved during his first hearing of the case to be told that Jesus was a Galilean and therefore came under Herod's jurisdiction. He at once sent Jesus off to Herod (Luke 23:5–12).

Herod had heard reports of Jesus's doings in the Galilee region and was curious about his miracles. He wanted Jesus to perform one in his presence.

When Jesus refused to answer questions or to oblige him by performing a miracle, Herod and his followers mocked and ill-treated Jesus and sent him back to Pilate.

In the meantime the priests had been busy whipping up demonstrations by their supporters and hinting to Pilate that they could easily arrange for the emperor, Tiberius, to hear about any leniency shown to a traitor wanting to supersede him as ruler of Palestine.

Pilate's questioning of Jesus convinced him that he was only dealing with a crank and that he was no danger to the state. He then made a serious error of judgment. He offered to release Jesus under the prevailing custom each Passover to amnesty and release a prisoner. By implication this suggested that he regarded Jesus as guilty and coming under the terms of the amnesty. The crowd vociferously rejected this offer and called loudly for the release of Barabbas, a local thug, convicted of riotous conduct.

Pilate then ordered Jesus to be flogged, perhaps in the hope that he might confess under torture or that the sight of him afterwards would arouse sympathy for him. Incited by the priests, the crowd bayed all the more loudly for his blood and shouted for his crucifixion. Finally, fearful of being stabbed in the back at Tiberias's court, Pilate weakly gave in. He publicly washed his hands of blame for Jesus's death and handed him over for execution.

It was the custom to scourge the condemned before crucifying them in order to weaken them and so hasten their death. Jesus may, therefore, have endured a second flogging. Matthew records (Matthew 27:29–31) that he was taken down to the Pretorium. There he was mocked and abused; an old red cloak was thrown over his bleeding shoulders, and a crown of thorns was forced down on his brow. He was then led off with the two condemned thieves to the place of execution.

On the way, Jesus stumbled and fell. The guards tried to whip him to his feet, but he was too weak to carry the cross on which he was to be hung. (It is possible that he was only carrying the crossbeam of the cross and that the upright post was left in the ground for repeated use.) The guards compelled a bystander, Simon of Cyrene, to carry the load for him. Simon may well have protested over being forced to walk in the procession, as if he was a common criminal. As he walked beside Jesus, Simon must have looked at Jesus with pity, and Jesus must have looked at him with gratitude. Afterwards Simon must have remembered that look and the intensity of the Love that shone through it. The fact that his sons are mentioned by Mark (15:21–22) suggests that Simon and his sons were early Christians. How grateful Simon must then have been that he had helped his Master in his hour of need!

Other records indicate that there was in Jerusalem a charitable group of women, who showed kindness to people condemned to death. These may be the Daughters of Jerusalem, whom Jesus addressed on his way to execution (Luke 23:28–32) and whom Jesus warned about the terrible fate ahead of them. As none of the other Evangelists reported this incident, it is possible that it was a legend started after the fall of the city in AD 70.

When Jesus got to the place of execution, similar, or perhaps the same, women offered Jesus wine mingled with gall as a narcotic to help ease his pain. Jesus refused it, evidently wanting to maintain complete control over his senses as long as possible. The executioners then threw Jesus roughly on the ground, stripped off his clothing, and nailed him to the cross.

Under such torture, most people would have shrieked in agony, pleaded for mercy, or abused the executioners. All Jesus could think about was the appalling sin of those killing him. With all the strength at his disposal he prayed: "Father, forgive them; they know not what they do" (Luke 23:33–34).

Most religious paintings of the scene show Jesus stretched out on the cross with his legs straight and his body under tension. Relics have been found that suggest that the victims of crucifixion were nailed to the cross with their legs bent. The fiendish cruelty of crucifixion lay in the fact that when the weight of the body was on the arms, suffocation set in. To ease this, the victim had to push up with his legs to take the weight off his arms. Victims thus suffered constant agony from wrists and ankles as they shifted their weight to and fro. In the end, to bring about death, the executioners used to break the legs of the victims to bring about their death through suffocation.

In a way, Pilate had the last laugh. He had a notice nailed to Jesus's cross indicating that Jesus was the king of the Jews. By implication this proclaimed the power of Rome and that the Jewish establishment, which had brought about Jesus's execution, sided with Rome.

As Jesus hung there, the bystanders jeered and taunted him, telling him to save himself if he was the Messiah (Luke 23:39–43). One of the thieves joined in with them. The other rebuked him and said to Jesus: "Remember me, when you come into your kingdom." To this Jesus replied: "In truth I tell you, today you will be with me in Paradise." How the spectators must have jeered. A dying felon talking about his kingdom! Yet the thief's words must have been such a comfort to Jesus. His conversion was a sign of what was to come and was the first fruit of his Passion. That very day the thief was to be in heaven with Jesus. No talk of purgatory. No talk of atonement for past sin. What a comfort to us!

In the crowd there were a few friends of Jesus and a small group of women with his mother and the Apostle John. John reports (John 19: 25–27) that Jesus, wishing to spare his mother sight of his last agonies, asked John to take her home and to look after her. This John did.

During the remaining hours of Jesus's agony on the cross there was some sort of eclipse or storm, and it grew dark. The three victims hung in the gloom, stinking of sweat, urine, and excrement, with flies buzzing over their bloody backs, wrists, and ankles. At some stage (Matthew 27:45–50) Jesus cried: "My God, my God, why have you forsaken me?" Jesus might have been trying to occupy his mind with memories of the psalms and been comforting himself with the twenty-second psalm. But perhaps he was at that moment experiencing the dark night of the soul, an experience which seems to come to mystics seeking at-onement with God. They have to experience the horror of hell, where God is not present, in order to understand the joy of heaven, of being in God's presence. In the same way, we have to know ugliness to know beauty, hate to know Love, and discord to know harmony. For Jesus to enter into that dark night would have been a terrible experience. He would have been momentarily sundered in two psychologically, as his human and divine natures were wrenched apart.

John records (John 19:28–30) that Jesus said he was thirsty. After someone gave him a drink of sour wine, he said: "It is fulfilled" and died. He had done all that he had come into the world to do and had done it to perfection. There was no more to do in this life. Luke 23:44–46 reports that Jesus's last words were: "Father, into your hands I commend my spirit." This was an indication that he had emerged from his dark night and was dying at one with the Father.

John reports (John 19:31–37) that later in the day the Jews wanted the bodies removed, so that they would not desecrate the Sabbath. It was ironic and revealing that they should have been so concerned about that relatively minor desecration, when they themselves had desecrated the Passover by committing the worst crime ever perpetrated, the Son's murder by spurious judicial action. They asked Pilate to have the three men's legs broken so that they would die quickly and could be removed. When the executioners came to do this, they found that Jesus was already dead. They therefore did not break his legs, but one of them pierced Jesus's body in the side with his spear. Only Luke reports (Luke 23:47–49) that the centurion in charge of the execution squad wondered over what had happened and saw in Jesus an innocent victim.

Meanwhile, Joseph of Arimathaea, a member of the Sanhedrin, who had been too scared to come out openly for Jesus, and Nicodemus, who had likewise feared to be known as a supporter of Jesus (John 3:1–21), begged his body off Pilate (John 19:38–42) and gave it decent burial in an unused tomb nearby. Later (Mark 27:42–46) the priests told Pilate about Jesus's prophecy that he would return and had the tomb sealed and placed under guard.

It is impossible to imagine fully the feelings that evening and the next day of Jesus's mother and closest friends. They had not only seen their loved one killed in the cruelest way; they had had their hopes dashed and their trust in Jesus shattered. Their sorrow and disillusionment must have been complete.

Chapter 7

Jesus's Resurrection

Jesus's death was not the end of the story. The unbelievable happened. Jesus was resurrected. He was not, like Lazarus, restored to normal life on earth (John 11:1–44). He had escaped the limitations of his earthly body and returned to the Godhead, from which he had come. He had retained his personality as it had been on earth, and his former material body had somehow been transmuted into something wholly spiritual. To human eyes, those of the people to whom he appeared, he was visible as the person he had been. Yet what was seen of his body did not observe the rules of matter. It could appear and disappear at will and transcended the limitations of space and time.

The idea that a person could be resurrected was as unbelievable then as it is now. Indeed, it should be more believable now. We have discovered so many things about the universe, which became believable only a few centuries or less ago. The big bang is beyond our comprehension. Science cannot penetrate behind it or explain it. Our imagination cannot conceive how a nut-sized object could explode and become the vast canopy of stars that we see at night. Nor can the average person understand how our physicists work out how that first explosion created matter, as we see it. We have to accept the discoveries of our scientists when our knowledge of the facts of matter supports their theories, and we have to change our ideas when new knowledge no longer supports a concept and forces a rethink.

So it is with Christ's resurrection. We have to accept it as an act of faith.

We have to look at what we do know and use that as a basis for our faith. The Evangelists report how the women went to the grave and found the tomb empty. They then rushed back to tell the apostles what they had discovered. How natural! The story has the ring of truth about it. So does the story about Peter and John's race to the tomb (John 20:1–10). It was in keeping with Peter's impulsive nature that he should rush in, and with John's reflective character that he should be first to draw the conclusion. It was in keeping with Mary Magdala's love of Jesus that she should have returned to the tomb and there seen Jesus and at first seen in him a gardener (John 20:11–18). Luke 22:13–35 tells how two disciples returning to Emmaus from Jerusalem met Jesus on the road and invited him in for supper. During their conversation Jesus explained how his passion fulfilled past prophecies. When he distributed the bread at the meal, they recognized who he was, and he disappeared. They were so convinced by their experience that they rushed the seven miles back to Jerusalem to tell the apostles what had happened. Who could have invented the stories (John 20:19–29) about how Jesus appeared to the apostles and how doubting Thomas at first refused to believe that Jesus could possibly have been resurrected and how he reacted, when he did?

It seems unbelievable that all these stories were invented by the Evangelists or imagined by people, who started legends through gossip that they had heard. The Evangelists had no motive deliberately to lie. Their allegiance to Jesus promised to bring them nothing but persecution and possible martyrdom. They would have had to be monumental hypocrites to promote deliberate falsehoods when they were preaching the ways of Love and Truth.

The most convincing evidence seems the fact that the grieving, disillusioned, and demoralized members of Jesus's team suddenly became the enthusiastic upholders of his claims and were so convincing that, despite the opposition of the Jewish and Roman establishments, they created a religion, which is now global, and the name of Jesus Christ is better known than any other. This is a fact, seemingly miraculous, which cannot be denied!

Perhaps the least bad reason for questioning the resurrection of Jesus is the paucity of information about what Jesus did and said during the weeks before his ascension. Matthew 28:16–20 tells of a meeting in the hills of Galilee, when Jesus commissioned the disciples to go out in the name of the Trinity, but this seems like a later addition to his Gospel, since it took nearly four hundred years before the concept of the Trinity was accepted by the church. Luke 24:44–49 mentions another commissioning. In an epilogue to his Gospel (perhaps added years later by someone else) John tells how Jesus met the apostles on the shore of Lake Galilee, had breakfast with them, and gave Peter a threefold command to feed his sheep, as if to absolve Peter of his threefold denial of him outside the Sanhedrin court (Mark 14:26–31 and 66–72).

It seems extraordinary that none of the apostles was recorded as having questioned Jesus about the manner of his resurrection and about conditions in heaven, or about points connected with his past teaching and prophecies, and that so little was reported of his doings during the time between his resurrection and ascension. Perhaps Jesus was silent about afterlife because their time- and space-bound minds could not comprehend anything he could say. None of this seems to invalidate the evidence for Jesus's resurrection.

Chapter 8

Jesus's Ascension and Pentecost

The Evangelists provide little information about how the time of Jesus's appearances ended. John mentions two sayings of Jesus before his death (John 6:63 and 20:17), which suggest that Jesus might have foreseen the manner of his departure, but he does not mention the actual event. Matthew merely mentions Jesus's final commission to the apostles. Mark 16:14–20 says that he was taken up to heaven, while having a meal with the apostles, at which time he gave them their final commission. Luke, in his Gospel (Luke 24:50–52), uses more or less the same words but places the event outside Bethany. Later (Acts 1:9), Luke writes that Jesus was lifted up while the disciples looked on until he was hidden by a cloud. According to Luke that ended the forty-day period during which Jesus appeared to his followers.

When reporting Jesus's baptism, John (John 1:34) notes that the Baptist foretold that Jesus would baptize with the Holy Spirit. Later John (John 14:16–18 and 26, 15:26, and 16:7–8) records Jesus's promise to send the apostles the Holy Spirit to encourage and support them and to lead them to Truth. Only Luke reports that this promise was repeated (Acts 1:8) just before Jesus's ascension and was fulfilled later (Acts 2:1–15) when the apostles, Jesus's mother, and some other female followers were together in Jerusalem. Something significant then happened. Luke described it as the sound of a gale, followed by tongues of fire settling on the heads of those present. Immediately they seemed consumed with energy and zeal.

As Luke was not there and was relying decades later on hearsay reports, we cannot be confident that his description of events is meant to be taken literally. In the two millennia since then, many people have experienced unitary knowledge of God. In talking about it, such mystics have used terms such as fire and light. In our day-to-day conversations we talk about people being fired with enthusiasm and zeal.

John 14:20 reports that Jesus had said that on the day of Pentecost they would know that he was in the Father and that they would be in him and he would be in them. Some fifteen hundred years later, Teresa of Avila would bring those words to life. She told her nuns that theirs, and by implication those of other people infused by Christ's personality, were the limbs that the resurrected Christ had on earth. She could have added mind and will. Today the same is true. People indwelt by the resurrected Christ and inspired by the Holy Spirit are the limbs and minds through which Christ works. He, not the Scriptures, is the Word made Flesh. The people "in him," the members of his Mystical Body, are his mouthpiece. His message is not frozen in ancient concepts and language. It is evolving, as people and their powers of understanding evolve. The fact that the whole of God's material creation is evolving should convince us of that.

In the realm of matter, the mutations, which play such a part in evolution, seem to work from the bottom up and not from the top down. We must expect the evolution of Christ's Mystical Body to evolve in the same way. Humble individuals, such as Francis of Assisi and Dame Julian of Norwich and other saintly people known and unknown, have been and will continue to be the organs of change.

Part 2

Christ's Teaching

Chapter 9

Christ's Revelation of God

If we accept the findings of science, we must accept too that the Genesis account (chapter 1) of creation no longer fits the facts. As Teilhard de Chardin concluded in his book *The Phenomenon of Man*, the birth of the human personality after millennia of gestation marked the appearance of a new phenomenon on the evolutionary scale. Unlike all that had gone before, the human personality has no length, no height, no breadth, and no weight and does not obey, as matter does, the rules of time and space. When describing people as made in the image of God (Genesis: 1:27), the writer of Genesis was inspired.

Centuries before people began to attribute to God the force of Love, and millennia before they had discovered atomic energy, they could not understand why God had created the human race and thought of God as a super tyrant ruler, who created people to amuse and work for him.

Francis of Assisi understood how Love creates itself through its outpouring and that lovers' capacity to Love grows with their use of it. Only people of our era can think in nuclear terms, and only after Jesus was it possible to think in the terms of the Trinity as a triune God. Using nuclear reaction, a feature of his creation, as a clue to him, we can see how a God of one person could hardly be a fountain of Love. We can imagine too how God's three persons pour out Love on each other and in so doing enhance the power of Love. We can believe that God took so much joy in the process that he wanted to extend it to a being outside himself and so created our race. Having done that, he had to reveal himself to us so that we knew what to love. The incarnation of the Son was his way of doing this. He injected his personality into our collective personality, thereby, as it were, injecting a spiritual gene into people and thereby empowering them to love as he loves.

To love as he loves they had to have free will to choose whether to love or not to love. As they evolved out of their past bestial state of acting by instinct, they had to ponder and reflect, to use their free will and to choose between good and evil and loving and not loving. There was no Garden of Eden save the bliss of ignorance in acting by instinct. There was no fall of Adam and Eve under the tree of knowledge. There was the beginning of our race's often painful ascent up the tree of evolution.

Of our time- and space-bound intellect, we cannot understand the spiritual ground of our being. The most comprehensive and understandable terms that God could use for his self-revelation were the terms of his Son's perfectly lived human life. Jesus made this clear when Philip (John 14) asked him to show the apostles the Father. He answered that anyone who had seen him had seen the Father. The same answer was implicit in Jesus's reply to Thomas (John 14:6–7) that he was the Way, the Truth, and the Life. He was the Way in that his life was a model to be followed and provided a track to run on. He was the Truth because his entire life was a revelation of Truth. He was the Life because the human personality/soul is totally dependent on acceptance of his presence within. He also described himself as the gate of the sheepfold (John 10:7) in that access to heaven is available through him.

Jesus's revelation of the Father was not a one-time event. It is a continuing event, as the resurrected Christ infuses people's minds with his, and new perspectives help us to understand better. His use of Abba, the equivalent of Daddy to us, conjures up the intimate relationship between a child and the best of fathers. It took fourteen hundred years before Julian of Norwich concluded that God does not know wrath and that, because his Love toward us is unchanging, his attitude toward us must also be unchanging. Therefore, forgiveness does not come into his relationship with us. He is like the father in the parable of the prodigal son (Luke 15:11–32). He loved the son all the time that he was away and embraced him in that same love on his return. It is we who project our anger with ourselves onto God, when we should be picking up the Love on offer, repenting, forgiving ourselves, and putting right what we did wrong. Jesus's remark about the unforgivable sin of speaking against the Holy Spirit (Matthew 12:22–32) is not an observation on

God's forgiving and a contradiction of Julian. It is an observation on people. If they are Satanists, deliberately call black white and white black, worship Satan and decry God, and have no love in them, they condemn themselves. They cannot abide heaven or the light of God's presence. They sense themselves to be totally incompatible with both and rush off to the hell of nothing out of which they were created, or perhaps they suddenly see that they have been long dead spiritually and that with the death of their body they are no more. This is not an end that God wills, but there is nothing that he can do about it, since there is no love in them on which he can get a grip, and their will is set against accepting his Love on offer.

Other parables may at first reading suggest otherwise—that Jesus preached a God of wrath and vengeance. Jesus was adept at tuning his message to his audience, and his audience mostly conceived of God as a traditional tyrant, who rewarded those who pleased him, punished ferociously those who did not, and wrought vengeance on his enemies. To appeal to his audience, Jesus set his parables in that setting, but their message lies in their core story and not their setting. Thus the point of the parable of the prodigal son lies in his portrayal of the father, not of the elder brother. The father epitomizes the unchanging and unconditional Love of God. He illustrates how God operates.

Chapter 10

The Kingdom of Heaven

Mark 1:15 tells us that from the outset of his public ministry Jesus preached about the kingdom of heaven and warned that it was close at hand. This warning was at first interpreted as a warning that the end of the world and the Day of Judgment were imminent. As the years passed it came to be seen more as a warning to individuals. Their moment of death might come at any time and would be their day of judgment, as they came face to face with God and judged themselves by their attitude to him and his heaven of Love.

Jesus had to use the term "kingdom," because his audience could not think in other terms. Tyrants of one sort or another ruled everywhere. Democracy was a concept that people did not know.

With all the benefits of scientific knowledge we try to see God through his creation from a perspective unknown two millennia ago. Today our physicists have plunged into theories about matter that are unintelligible to the average person, for example, the quantum understanding of matter. This suggests that all matter is at bottom particles of energy, which have relationships with each other and are held in their state of being by various forces, such as gravity, the strong and weak forces, and other still undiscovered forces. This concept of matter provides a clue to an insight into the state of heaven. Heaven is not a monarchy, and monarchies nowadays are mostly discredited forms of government. Heaven is rather a state of being and of relationships. It is a form of existence, where all who have being are souls in a state of harmony centered on God and maintained in being by the force of Love, which is God. It is against that background that we need to reflect on the resurrected Jesus's teaching, remembering that his teaching two millennia ago was subject to the limitations of the manhood, which he had voluntarily accepted.

Jesus indicated (Luke 17:20–21) that the state of heaven does not admit of observation. No one will be able to say: "Look, there it is!" It is among people. It is the spiritual ground of our being. It is what people are meant to focus on above all else (Matthew 6:35). It is possible to attain that state of harmony during life on earth (Luke 9:27), and the dying thief on the cross beside Jesus was promised entry into it that very day. Essentially, being in heaven is being in harmony with its state of existence and at one with the force, God/Love, which keeps it in being.

Jesus spent much time and energy in helping his followers to understand what heaven is about. It is clearly not a place of luxury and pleasure and sex (Matthew 22:30), as envisioned by parts of the book of Revelation or Muslim concepts of paradise. Jesus used some of his most colorful language in talking about it. He likened it to:

1. a grain of mustard seed: great networks of loving relationships grow out of a spark of Love (Matthew 13:31);
2. a germinating seed: as a seed grows on its own in soil, provided that it is watered, so does Love in the individual, when nurtured by Grace through the power of Jesus and the Holy Spirit (Mark 4:26–29);
3. yeast: Love permeates the receptive personality and causes it to develop, as yeast permeates dough and causes it to rise (Matthew 13:33);
4. hidden treasure: the person who finds it recognizes it and acts accordingly (Matthew 13:44);
5. a pearl merchant: the collective personality of those in heaven is ever on the watch for new, graceful people to draw into its embrace, and, conversely, the pearl to the finder is like the treasure in the field (Matthew 13:45–46);
6. a net: God's network of Love is ever seeking to capture more people but inevitably excludes the people who are loveless and incompatible with it (Matthew 12:47);

7. a householder bringing new and old things out of his store: Jesus's vision of heaven drew on the vision of seers before him but also put forward new ideas (Matthew 13:52);

8. a farmer who sowed good seed that an enemy polluted with weeds: heaven exists while both good and evil flourish in people; they have the free will to choose between the two, but the time of harvest will come when Love will reap the loving into its system and let the loveless exclude themselves (Matthew 13:24–30); and

9. a king who settled accounts with his servants: the loveless are incompatible with the loving, and, using God-given talents as he intended them to be used, is a matter of loving (Matthew 18:23–35).

As indicated by the parable of the ten bridesmaids (Matthew 25:1–13), the day of reckoning will be sprung upon us: we none of us know when we shall be drawn through death's portal and come face to face with God. It is thus vital that we should cultivate a relationship with him now so that he has something to cling to in us, when in shame over our past we may seek to flee his presence.

The creation of a relationship of love with God is of the greatest urgency to time-bound people, but time creates no precedence in God's sight, c.f. Jesus's remarks about the first being last and the last first (Mark 10:31) and the parable about the laborers in the vineyard (Matthew 20:1–16).

Chapter 11

Jesus's Two Commandments

Matthew 22:34–40 tells how a Pharisee asked, "Which is the greatest commandment of the law?" Jesus replied, "You must love the Lord your God with all your heart, with all your soul, and with all your mind." This is the greatest and the first commandment. The second is like it: "You must love your neighbor as yourself."

In answer to the question, "Who is my neighbor?" Jesus told the beautiful parable about the Good Samaritan (Luke 10:29–37).

In his magnificent paean to Love (1 Corinthians 13) St. Paul beautifully described Love, and his cry, "I live; yet not I, for Christ lives in me" (Galatians 2:20), echoes down the centuries in everyone who has felt the infection of the resurrected Christ's personality.

St. Augustine of Hippo summed it up when he said, "Love and do what you will."

The old adage "It's Love that makes the world go round" is true in that God has, through Jesus, revealed himself as Love, and Love is the force that holds the realm of the spirit, the state of heaven, together and in being.

The traditional seven virtues—prudence, temperance, fortitude, justice, faith, hope, and charity—are all the fruits of Love. The seven deadly sins—pride, covetousness, lust, envy, gluttony, anger, and sloth—are the fruits of excluding Love. They are deadly because they ensure that self displaces Love and kills the soul by depriving it of sustenance.

How important it thus is to be greedy for Grace, the power to love as God loves, and to importune God with requests for it!

Chapter 12

Prayer

The Evangelists record that Jesus told his disciples not to pray like the pagans using many words and flowery language but to pray like this: "Our Father in heaven, holy be your name, your kingdom come, your will be done on earth as it is in heaven. Give us today our daily bread. And forgive us our offenses as we forgive others theirs. Lead us not into temptation, but save us from evil."

In some ways this prayer is like a mantra. It can be repeated many times over and get people into the mood really to pray. It is also a model prayer to be used as a standard structure for both communal and personal prayer.

To pray we need to put ourselves in the presence of God and recollect to whom we are talking. The words "Our Father in heaven" do that beautifully. "Our" reminds us that we share God as Father with everyone else. We are one big spiritual family, in which all are our brothers and sisters. We are all equally loved by God, and that family is a spiritual family in the state of heaven, where all have relationships of Love with each other and with God, on whom all is centered.

"Hallowed be your name" cannot be our prayer unless we are full of awe in thinking of our Creator and the marvels of his creation. We therefore need to cultivate a sense of awe, and this phrase should help us do so.

"Your Kingdom come" puts us on the spot. We cannot pray these words honestly if we do nothing to help bring forward the day when the state of heaven extends over the whole earth.

"Your Will be done." It is useless saying these words unless we make an effort to understand what God's will/purpose is. That necessitates prayerful meditation on what Jesus taught as recorded in the Gospels and what the resurrected Christ has been teaching over the past two millennia. To hear the teaching of the resurrected Christ we have to listen to what he has been saying through saintly Christians, the people who have best allowed him to dwell in them and to act through them.

"Give us this day our daily bread" is generally interpreted as the food and drink we need to stay alive and perform our vocation. It also includes the other things (e.g., talents, knowledge, health, and Grace to carry out that vocation). As my mother said to me when I joined the diplomatic service and doubted whether I had the qualities to succeed: "If that is your vocation, you can count on God to give you what you need. He will not ask you to do a job and not give you the tools to do it."

"Forgive us our offenses as we forgive others theirs" indicates that we must not ask God to do things for us that we are not prepared to do for others. The parable of the unforgiving debtor (Matthew 18:23–35) was an awful warning to people who expect to be forgiven but do not forgive.

"Lead us not into temptation" strikes me as oddly worded, because God would hardly lead us into temptation. He may well lead us into situations in which we are tested. When we are tempted by the forces of evil (e.g., by sexual fantasies) it is often pleasurable to dally with them. That is the moment to ask to be led out of the temptation, interpreting "not into" as "out of."

"Deliver us from evil" is a cry for help. We feel in the grip of forces too strong for us.

Jesus promised that if we prayed in his name to the Father, the Father would grant our request (John 16:23–24). Praying in his name implies letting him inspire the prayer and, as it were, pray through us.

Luke reports (Luke 11:5–13) the need to ask, even though God knows before we ask, what we need. In the parables of the importunate friend (Luke 11:5–8) and of the judge and the importunate widow (Luke 18:1–8) Jesus emphasizes the importance of asking, because asking conditions the will to receive. People asking for forgiveness from God, even though they know God's Love is unchanging toward them, need to condition their own mind to repentance and to forgiving themselves and putting right the wrong they have done.

In his Gospel, John included long accounts of Jesus's thoughts and prayers. These sound as if they were more summaries of John's recollections long after the event than verbatim accounts of what Jesus actually said. It seems that at the time of temptation, on the Mount of Transfiguration and in the Garden of Gethsemane, Jesus's prayer was a laying out of his problems before God rather than a series of requests. Apart from Jesus's prayers for the disciples (John 17), he does not seem to have used much supplication on behalf of other people and their needs in his prayers; nor is there that sort of clause of supplication in the Lord's Prayer. The impression given by the Evangelists is that for Jesus prayer was primarily a sharing of thoughts and experience with the Father. The small boy who went off to the Lady Chapel in church to tell God a pirate story while his mother did the flowers, was following Jesus's example in communing with the Father.

The old adage that work is prayer is very true when the work is done to the best of one's ability out of Love of God. Both Therese of Lisieux and Brother Lawrence provide good examples of this.

John reported that the soul needs both food and drink to survive and that Jesus indicated to the Samaritan woman that his drink was communion with the Father (John 4:10–24) and, later, that his soul's food was action in accordance with the Father's will (verse 34). The same must assuredly be true for us.

Communal prayer should also, I believe, follow the structure of the Lord's Prayer, and its liturgy should evolve in tune with the evolution of people's knowledge and thinking. If we believe that God's Love is always and unconditionally on offer to people and that he is always wanting to do his best for individuals, there seems no point in asking him to act. The point of asking lies in the conditioning of the will to accept. When I pray for an individual, I hope that telepathy in some way affects the will of the person for whom I pray, who is personally known to me. To me the sweeping prayers in, for example, the prayers for the people in Anglican liturgies are pointless, where I have no personal contact with the people prayed for and can do nothing for them and where telepathy can hardly play any part in the process; nor can I see any evidence that Jesus prayed in that way.

Jesus instituted the sacrament of the eating and drinking of bread and wine in remembrance of him and taught that the essential food and drink of the soul is carrying out the will of his Father and enjoying communion with the Father. This should be the theme of services of public worship, and they should be structured around it and the form of the Lord's Prayer. It was natural for the first Jewish converts to Christianity, to structure their services on their traditional forms of worship. Tradition and the past are good to keep in mind, since experience is a good teacher, but they should not be allowed to put blinkers on people's vision or to cramp their thinking. For too long the church has been towing tradition as a yacht tows a dinghy, which impedes its progress. It is time for the church to cut the tow rope and evolve a liturgy that holds to the thinking of the resurrected Christ and is in tune with it, as manifested by the people in whom Christ has dwelt and now dwells.

I have no expert knowledge on which to base views on the liturgy. All I do know is that, if I try to concentrate on it during a service, I find that my thoughts are distracted by my disagreement with the words being uttered, and if I do not concentrate on them I daydream. I expect that that is true of other people. At the risk of being thought intellectually impertinent, I attach at Appendix A my own cockshy draft. I hope that, in shying at it, liturgists will evolve better ideas.

Chapter 13

Evil and Suffering

Jesus, like the Jews, believed in a personal devil, the source of all evil, the counterpart to God and God's opponent in the fight to win souls for Love. Belief in that sort of being raises unanswerable questions about its origin.

The Jews saw Satan as a fallen angel, who had rebelled against God and been expelled from his presence. To us the devil can be regarded as the collective personality of people without Love in them. People who are loveless and full of hatred collect around them people of like mind and try to attract others to them in their pursuit of self. As people developed out of the bestial state of acting by instinct and increasingly acted through reason and conscious choice, some of them consciously chose to follow the path of evil in pursuit of self. They thus formed a collective personality of evil, and that seems very much the devil of the twenty-first century AD.

Yet, dreadful things happen to people that are not the result of human sin. The way in which God created our universe causes disasters to happen (e.g., volcanic eruptions, earthquakes, tsunamis, and hurricanes). It has become common for people to attribute both bad and good experiences to God's will as punishments for sin or rewards for good behavior. Babies and toddlers are often victims of natural disasters. A just and loving God could not possibly be punishing them. If a drunk driver kills a toddler, the child's death seems clearly an act of evil, the result of sin, and contrary to God's will. Illnesses such as Alzheimer's and Lou Gehrig's are a feature of what exists as a result of

God's creation being what it is, but God can hardly be charged with willing them.

Jesus did touch on this problem. John 9:1–3 records that the disciples saw a man who had been born blind and asked Jesus who had sinned, he or his parents. Jesus answered that the man was born blind so that the works of God might be displayed in him. The words "so that" can be understood as "purposefully" or "consequentially." If God ensured that the man was born blind to give Jesus the opportunity to perform his miracle, that act seems hardly compatible with God's loving nature. If the man was born blind with the result that Jesus had the opportunity to cure him, that raises the question of chance.

Luke 12:1–5 reports that on another occasion Jesus was told about the killing by the Romans of some Galileans and about the death of other people through the collapse of the Tower of Siloam. He commented that it was wrong to think of those who had died as greater sinners than those who had survived, but he warned that similar disasters would occur if people did not repent and change their ways.

Matthew 11:3 tells that Jesus forecast the fall of the thriving town of Capernaum and said that Sodom would not have been destroyed had its people seen the miracles that Capernaum had witnessed.

John 11:3–15 reports that Jesus deliberately delayed answering Martha and Mary's appeal for help until after Lazarus's death. Here Jesus caused the sisters much temporary anguish by seizing the opportunity to perform a sensational miracle that was bound to worry the priests in Jerusalem. The joy that this brought the sisters must far have outweighed their first sorrow and enormously increased their faith in and Love of Jesus.

From these reports it seems reasonable to conclude that Jesus did not worry so much about the causes of suffering as concern himself with what should be done about it. In individually and collectively tackling that question out of Love of our neighbor, we shall be effecting God's purposes and extending the power of Love.

Jesus does not appear to have discussed with the disciples the unfairness of life or the uneven part that chance plays in individuals' lives. Some people seem so lucky; others seem so unlucky. Christian dogma has often assumed that there can be no such thing as chance, because nothing can happen outside God's control. Here evolution seems to have a message for us. Mutations leading to evolutionary progress have played an essential role in the creation of our race and are evidently part of the mechanism, which God established, to bring about what he wanted to achieve. To create a creature capable of loving as he loves, he had to create a creature with free will. If everything in life were planned by him, there would be no opportunity for people to have real freedom of choice. Chance thus appears the element in his creation that enabled God to stand back from it enough to grant people free will.

In the past people tended, and still often tend, to regard apparent episodes of good or bad luck as "God's will." It is illogical and almost blasphemous to regard the results of evil as God's will. Is it God's will that a drunk driver runs down a toddler? Or that an athlete or loving parent should get Lou Gehrig's or Alzheimer's diseases? That cannot be so. Moreover, the entire tenor of Jesus's way of Love as well as the message of the parable of the Good Samaritan (Luke 10:29–37) is that every disaster and mishap should be regarded as an opportunity for the use and outpouring of Love. It is God's purpose that we should also work tirelessly to remove as far as possible the causes of evil (e.g., through research and social change).

Chapter 14

The Parables and Jesus's Personality

Most people have some trait that is, as it were, their trademark, by which they can be instantly recognized. Jesus's trademark was his parables. They sum up his teaching. Only a person of genius with the imagination of a poet could have come up with such a variety of apposite stories. To analyze them all would require a much lengthier tome than this book is intended to be. The best way to deal with them is to make them individually subjects of prayerful meditation. They then not only reveal insights into Jesus's teaching but also into his personality. They become infectious. Just as people infect us with laughter and sadness and fire us with enthusiasm and zeal, the parables, under the inspiration of the resurrected Christ and Holy Spirit, help to infect us with the personality of Christ and to see him as a whole. They validate the four portraits of Jesus by the Evangelists as evidence that he was a fact of history.

Jesus's reasons for talking in parables were set out in his explanation of the parable of the sower (Matthew 13:1–23). The stories were intended to be easy to remember and to make people think.

Jesus's parables are set in the context of his times. Thus where kings and powerful men appear in his stories and might be regarded as symbolizing God, they do not portray God as Jesus revealed him. The father in the parable of the prodigal son was the loving dad of Jesus's experience, and he himself was the Good Shepherd (John 10:1–18).

Jesus was no sentimental "softie" or wimp. He was a tough leader of people. He was tough on himself and tough on his followers and was ready to live the life of a tramp, if need be. When he wanted to, he could and did act the demagogue and sway crowds.

Only a person of great force of personality could have dominated the merchants in the temple precincts and created mayhem in their market and gotten away with it.

The way in which he planned the final crunch between him and the Jewish establishment revealed that he had great strength of purpose and could be skillfully calculating and manipulative.

He obviously enjoyed being with people and loved a party and was accused by his enemies of being a drunkard (Matthew 11:19). Yet he was no simple extrovert but needed frequent communion between himself and the Father.

He could be harsh with his closest friends and was angered when the disciples officiously tried to take him away from children (Mark 10:13–16), and he called Peter Satan (Mark 8:33), when Peter rebuked him for defeatist talk.

He could also be tender, as when he lamented over Jerusalem (Matthew 23:37–39). Only a person with an eye for the beauty of God's creation could have talked of a hen gathering her chicks under her wing or of wildflowers as having a beauty greater than Solomon's in all his finery. He had a propensity always to look on the bright side of things. An old legend relates that once, when walking along the road, he and his disciples came across the body of a dog. The disciples walked by holding their noses and muttering about the stink. Jesus merely remarked on the beautiful whiteness of its teeth. When he talked about God's care of his creation (Luke 12:23–32) and the need to trust in providence, he made no mention of how red nature is in tooth and claw. In his day people seem to have had no interest in their environment. There is no evidence that Jesus was environmentally inclined in the modern sense of the words.

Jesus used to exaggerate to ram home a point that he wanted to impress on his audience or to be remembered. When warning people not to judge others (Matthew 7:1–5), the brother who wanted to remove a splinter from his brother's eye was said to have a plank in his. When talking about the danger of riches (Matthew 19:23–26), Jesus said it was easier for a camel to go through the eye of a needle than for a rich man to enter heaven.

The parable of the talents (Matthew 25:14–30) is a graphic lesson in the need to use one's talents. Using them increases their productivity, and neglecting them causes them to wither away. This results in those using them most effectively gaining most. In the mind of the audience, the disappointed master would indeed have cast out the lazy servant. In God's world the servant would have excluded himself because of his sense of shame and incompatibility with the master's household. The parable also reminds us that we hold our talents, and indeed everything else, including our environment, in trust.

In his teaching, Jesus had emphasized that timing had no relevance in people's entry into heaven. The parable of the laborers in the vineyard (Matthew 20:1–16) illustrates this, as did Jesus's promise to the good thief on the cross: despite a lifetime of crime the thief was going to be that day in heaven. The way in which the owner of the vineyard paid the last first and made those who had worked longest wait longest seemed calculated to enrage the workers but would have caused the parable to be noted and remembered.

In telling the story of the crafty steward (Luke 16:1–9), Jesus was not advising people to be dishonest like the steward but to use their brains in God's service as the dishonest did in the service of their own interests.

The parables also indicate Jesus's gift of repartee. He was adept at producing quick and devastating answers to points raised by his critics in argument. How remarkable that he could think up the parable of the Good Samaritan in answer to the lawyer's question: Who is my neighbor? (Luke 10:29–37) and instantly produce such cunning answers to the priests' question about the source of his authority (Matthew 21:23–27) and to the Pharisees' question about paying tribute to Rome (Matthew 22:15–22).

Chapter 15

The Miracles

Matthew 16:1–4 reports that Pharisees and Saducees once approached Jesus and asked for a sign from heaven in support of him. In a typical down-to-earth reply, Jesus chided them for being able to interpret the signs of the weather but not being willing to interpret the signs of the times (by implication, what he was doing). He added that the sign they would get would be the sign of Jonah, who spent three days in the belly of the whale. This was an oblique prophecy to the period between his death and resurrection.

All four of the Evangelists clearly regarded Jesus's extraordinary acts of healing as miracles, and the apostles believed that they were. Jesus himself recognized his peculiar powers and regarded them as a gift from God to be used responsibly. Jesus had been tempted to use them on stunts but had rejected that temptation. When the Evangelists wrote, there were still people alive who had witnessed what had happened and could vouch for the truth of their reports. Like Jesus's resurrection, his miracles cannot be confirmed and have to be taken on trust, but the Evangelists record many minor details of the circumstances of the miracles (e.g., Mark 2:1–12 about how a roof was stripped to let a paralyzed man down to Jesus to be cured), which can hardly have been imagined, that add to the credibility of the reports. Some miracles were performed on the Sabbath, e.g., the cure of the man with a withered hand (Mark 3:1–6), as support for Jesus's attack on the over rigid rules about resting on the Sabbath.

Some of the illnesses cured by Jesus may not have been what they seemed. People can mistake comas for death, minor skin diseases for incipient leprosy, and epileptic fits as something more sinister. We are beginning to understand psychiatric problems and know about the strange ways in which African witch doctors can, through curses and spells, bring about the death of their victims. Nothing can explain Lazarus's resuscitation. It was part of Jesus's plan to force a confrontation with the Jewish establishment and achieved its object. Its effect on the Pharisees and Sadducees suggests that something remarkable must have happened.

The story of the wedding feast (John 2:1–12), recorded as Jesus's first miracle, has about it a legendary character. The Evangelists give the impression that Jesus burst upon the Galilean scene at the start of his public ministry and quickly made a very big impression. The reports of those who attended the wedding and noticed the improvement in the wine would have spread like wildfire.

Even more so would have the reports of the two miracles of the feeding of the crowd (Matthew 14:13–21 and 15:32–39). Jesus had initially resisted the temptations to use his powers to create food or perform stunts. Like the raising of Lazarus, these two miracles were special signs that Jesus was what he claimed to be. John reports (John 6:14–15 and 49–58) that the immediate result was a rave reaction from the crowd. This is what Jesus must have anticipated. Immediately afterwards he launched into his discourses about his being food for the soul and poured cold water on the crowd's enthusiasm. His strange talk caused many disciples to stop following him. A friend of mine followed their example, objecting to the celebration of the Last Supper/ Eucharist/Mass on the ground of its cannibalistic language. John saw that these two miracles were signs to prepare for the institution of that sacrament.

Two recorded miracles sometimes puzzle people. These are the curing of the Syro-Phoenician woman (Mark 7:24–30) and that of the man called Legion (Luke 8:26–39). Could Jesus really have talked to the woman apparently so contemptuously? Perhaps she addressed him as if she wondered at his attitude in the light of Jewish arrogance toward Gentiles, and the loving and wry look in Jesus's eyes as he said what he did, told her what he thought about that attitude. Could Jesus really have caused a herd of pigs to run headlong into the lake and thereby perhaps have ruined the peasant who owned them? The local people perhaps needed such a sign to convince them that Legion was no longer possessed and could be let back in their community. In Jesus's sight, one man was worth more than a herd of pigs.

No amount of argument or evidence is going to convince the skeptic, who is determined not to believe. As with the parables, we can hope that prayerful meditation on the miracles will enable us to see in them the truth that those signs were meant to convey. As too with the Evangelists' portraits of Jesus, we need to get back to them to see what they were trying to convey. A book such as this can only provide a snapshot with a twenty-first century focus that may well distort the picture.

Chapter 16

Conclusion of Part 2

John first concluded his Gospel by saying that there were many other signs Jesus worked in the sight of the disciples that were not recorded by him. His purpose in writing about Jesus was to enable his readers to believe that Jesus is the Christ, the Son of God, and that through believing in him they might have life.

These words seem equally appropriate as the conclusion of Part 2 of this book. Its object is to give a credible pen portrait of Jesus as seen by a layperson of the twenty-first century. It is also my hope that it will prove infectious with the Love that made Jesus what he was.

Part 3

Conclusion of Book 2

If, dear reader, you have come thus far with me, you may have concluded that you are indeed part of God's Project People and have a role to play in it. These questions may then arise in your mind: what is your role, and what are you to do about it?

Over half a century ago, I decided on a practice of daily meditation and prayer, which has brought me to today. I could not have written this book fifty years ago. Its conclusions have seeped into my mind slowly over the years.

I have set out in my three books about seeking the Christ of AD2000 and in my "Spiritual Exercises for AD2000" the way in which my mind has worked. Looking back on the past, I have had the feeling that I have been led on to the conclusions that I have reached. I have recorded my thoughts not out of any sense of their importance but as coming from me and in the hope that they will evoke better thoughts and conclusions among others.

The facts of history seem to me to show that people have been evolving from a bestial state of acting out of instinct to a rational state of pondering and reflecting and acting out of Love. History also seems to show that people have a natural tendency to believe that there is some First Cause, or God, and to look upon him as their Creator and the Creator of all that exists. This belief has evolved as people have evolved and has been nurtured and developed under the influence of people inspired by their insights into the nature of God.

History has recorded that some two millennia ago Jesus claimed to be God's incarnated Son, sent into our world to reveal God's nature and purpose in our creation. History has also recorded that over that period belief in Jesus has become global and that more people believe in him than ever before. These seem facts that are as incontrovertible as, for example, evolution or the force of gravity.

Likewise, the facts suggest that a process of convergence is now obvious in the development of our human species. We are moving toward a global language, English. We now have a global pool of knowledge on the Internet, and rapidly developing communications are bringing increasing numbers of people into contact with each other.

The more I have thought and prayed about this, the more convinced I have become that God is willing our human race into convergence in at-onement with him, the goal of his "Project People." Yet, such at-onement is only possible if people want it, seek it, and allow God to bring it about through the force of the Love which he is.

The God in whom I believe will always be a mystery because he lies outside the limits of time and space and is beyond our comprehension. I believe that Jesus of Nazareth was God incarnate and through his life on earth and resurrection was and is God's self-revelation in the highest terms capable of being understood by the human mind. I also believe that his life on earth represented the end of the development of God's process for the creation of people with the potential to attain at-onement with him and to love as he loves.

To me, Jesus's life on earth was the watershed of God's "Project People." Before it people did not know enough about God really to love him. Afterwards they could know him, and the personality of the Son had been injected into the collective personality of our race. Now we have the potential to achieve that at-onement by letting the resurrected Christ and Holy Spirit direct our unique personality in acting out in Christ's Mystical Body of all believers the role for which God has designed us. How important it is that we Christians should hang on to our belief in that watershed by retaining BC and AD and rejecting the BCE and CE that unbelievers are now trying to foist upon us!

Over the past two millennia, there has been ample evidence of atrocities committed in the name of Christ by Christian churches and sects; and since the Reformation spawned an increasing number of Protestant Christian churches and sects, the cacophony of dissension in Christendom seems to have gotten louder. Yet, beneath the surface of organized Christendom the number of believers in the resurrected Christ has been increasing and now outnumbers those of any other religion. Whereas the establishments of Christendom mostly seem determined to maintain their disunity, Christian individuals increasingly work together on works of Love and seem to be evolving toward that at-onement with God and each other, which is the goal of God's Project People.

Over the past two millennia too there has been ample evidence about the ways in which individuals have sought at-onement with God, and people are now increasingly free to choose the way that appeals to them most. For many people the use of mantras has proved helpful in focusing the mind on God, and many mantras are available for choice. Personally, I created my own and for over fifty years have started my day with it. To me it has summed up what the Christian way of life should be about, and it has become the target at which I try to aim my will. It seems appropriate, therefore, that I should end this book by leaving it with you:

"Dearest Father in heaven, I look up to you in awe and love and gratitude for all the blessings of this life, and particularly for the gift of your Son to reveal you to me and to teach me to love as you love. May I be so infected with his personality and so inspired by your Holy Spirit that my will becomes your will and all my doing is powered by love."

Appendix A

Possible Form of Family Eucharist

Extract from chapter 5 of *Praying in the Mystical Body of the Christ of AD2000*

Any new liturgy should, I suggest, be built around:

1. The structure of the Lord's Prayer;
2. Jesus's two commandments to us to love God and our neighbor;
3. Jesus's teaching (recorded in the Fourth Gospel) that the drink of the soul is communion with God, and its food is action in accordance with God's Will; and
4. The belief that the resurrected Christ does dwell in people who believe in and accept him, and that the way to at-onement with God lies through his Son.

Having been taught in the diplomatic service that anyone suggesting something should put up a draft, I attach a rough sketch of the sort of family Eucharist I have in mind. It sums up the message of this book.

Family Eucharist

Part 1—The Welcome of the Priest or Leader

Priest: This house of God offers a warm welcome to us all.

We come here in the belief that it is the spark of God's spirit, with which we are endowed at birth, and the power of his Love within us that have brought us here. His Love is ever longing to hold us in its grasp. He wants us to commune and act communally, as well as individually, with him and thereby to increase our relationships of Love with him and with all his other children.

In coming here let us remember the throng of people, some known to us but most unknown, who have prayed within these walls and in afterlife now share with us the blessing of God's Grace and with God beam their Love on us. They are present with us here.

To our first-time visitors today, I bid a special welcome. If you are already Christians, we shall find our faith enhanced by your presence with us and hope that you will leave this place with yours enhanced as well. If you do not yet know the resurrected Christ, we hope that you will catch from us a longing to be at one with God in Love by absorbing and being absorbed by his personality.

Part 2—The Practice of the Presence of God

Priest: Let us now place ourselves in the presence of God.

Dearest Father in heaven, we look up to you in awe and love and gratitude. In awe we sense, albeit dimly, the wonder of what you are: Three persons in one God, where Father, Son, and Holy Spirit create the force of Love by pouring Love upon each other and reflecting it back enhanced to each other. In Love, because the capacity to love, which you have given us, has drawn us into the embrace of your Love. In gratitude for our creation and all the blessings of this life, and particularly for the gift of your Son to reveal you to us and to provide the means for us to reach our destiny in you.

People: Father, accept us in your presence here.

Priest: God has created us out of nothing to achieve at-onement with himself in Love. To love as he loves and to create as he creates, we must be free to love or not to love, to create or to destroy.

God has given us a personal identity, soul, or personality, which is, as it were, a spiritual embryo. During our life on earth it can grow through Love and become at one with God and achieve eternal life in him or, without Love, it can diminish into the void from which we came.

People: Father in heaven, give us Grace to love you more and to love our neighbor as our self. Catch us up in that network of loving relationships, which is your state of heaven about us and within.

Part 3—Knowledge of God's Will

Priest: To love God and to seek to act in harmony with his will, we must needs seek to know him better through our Love of his resurrected Son, the Word Made Flesh, and through people in whom the Son has dwelt and dwells. Let us now hear what the Evangelists have to say.

First Lesson: *Chosen verses from one of the Gospels.*

Priest *comments briefly.*

Let us also hear what saintly people, who have been indwelt by Christ and inspired by the Holy Spirit, have to say.

Second Lesson: *Either verses chosen from the rest of the New Testament or about some saintly person or from some enlightening Christian writing.*

Priest *comments briefly.*

Let us now remind ourselves of the creed that our Christian forbears have used for centuries, recognizing that, in the context of our age, we may see it in new light.

Priest *leads people in saying the Nicene Creed.*

Priest: Let us pray.

Father in heaven, we pray to you in Faith and Love, knowing that you will ever be a mystery to people on earth, but loving you because of your Love of us and the revelation of you, which Jesus effected by his life on earth and which the resurrected Christ enlarges through his Mystical Body. May our will be so inspired by Love through the power of the Holy Spirit that we in this life become a part of your heavenly network of relationships of Love. May we become so absorbed in the personality of your Son that we operate indeed as his mind, his voice, and his limbs.

People: Jesus, dear master and friend, here we are! Use us as you will.

Part 4—Confession

Priest: When we measure ourselves against the standards set by the perfect life of Jesus Christ, we see at once how far short we fall of the target that God has set for us. Let us reflect on the extent to which, since our last confession, we may have fallen short of what God would have us be. May we see clearly the extent to which we may have allowed our will at times to move us away from the upward path of Love and growth that leads to eternal life in God down onto the slippery slope of alienation from Love that leads to diminution and spiritual death.

People: *(after a period of silent reflection and led by the priest)*

Dearest Father in heaven, we know that your Love is always beamed on us and that you ever long to keep us in its embrace. Yet we have often offended against you. We have of our own free will acted without Love. We have done loveless deeds. We have acted without Love toward other people. We have thought loveless thoughts and enjoyed sexual and other temptations. We have at times been loveless, idle, and preoccupied with our own selfish interests. We have been in the grip of evil. We know, deep down, that, whatever the mitigating circumstances, we go through life in danger of losing our relationship with you and of being drawn away from you. May our sense of guilt and shame not cause us to want to escape from you and drive us away from you forever. Of your boundless generosity give us the Grace to turn our will and mind lovingly toward you. May your Son and Holy Spirit keep us moving forward toward at-onement with you. May we undo the harm we have done to others and genuinely repent, forgive ourselves, and accept the Love consistently and unconditionally on offer from you. May we be so in Love with your Love that our joy is ever in pleasing you. This we ask, knowing that it is what you want.

Priest: Through the power of Jesus Christ dwelling in you and under the inspiration of the Holy Spirit, may you cast away all feelings of alienation and of guilt that keep you from God. May you never project your anger with yourself onto him; and may you throw yourselves unreservedly on his unconditional and unchanging Love. You can indeed be confident that, if you let it, his Grace will rescue you from evil and bring you home to him.

Part 5—Food for the Soul

Priest: Did not Christ say that his spiritual food was doing the will of the Father? Our souls likewise need the food of action as well as the drink of prayer and communion with God. Let us pray together.

People led by **Priest:** Father in heaven, you have created us in your image to love and to create as you love and create and to extend the network of your state of heaven. Grant us the Grace to do as you would have us do and act out the unique role that you have in mind for each of us.

Priest: It is right that each of us should act in our unique way and to our own particular design and vocation, but our presence here reminds us that we are members of Christ's Mystical Body and, as such, units in a greater whole. Through our collective prayer and action we have a special role in strengthening the power of Love and extending heaven. Let us now review what, as a Christian community, we are doing. [*He reports on current activities.*] Has anyone any additional points to raise? Let us pray.

Jesus, our master and friend, during your life on earth you showed us how to act. Be our inspiration now. Help us, as cells in your Mystical Body, to act effectively as instruments of your Love in our community. Open our eyes to what needs to be done and to how we can be effective in your hands. Help us to concentrate our talents and resources to best effect, remembering that, in our desire to work together, we must not weaken our ability to carry out our personal vocation in your service.

People: Father in heaven, give us Grace to serve you through your Son.

Priest: Let us remember in our prayers the bereaved, the sick, and the dying and those in special need of Love in our community. In particular I ask you to pray for [*he mentions those known to him*]. Does anyone want to mention anyone else?

People: Father in heaven, we hold them up to the radiance of your Love. Show us what you want us to do to help.

Priest: The earth is full of people in distress and in want of Love and the necessities of life. In particular I am thinking of [*he names those recently in the news*] Let us hold them up in our imagination to the radiance of God's Love.

People: Father in heaven, we hold them up to you. Show us what you want us to do to help.

Priest: The miseries endured on earth are often the results of the actions of misguided and loveless people in the grip of evil. Let us pray that Love may seep into their thinking and turn malevolence to Love.

People: Father in heaven, may we do what we effectively can do to spread the influence of your Love and make the world more like heaven.

Priest: The miseries occasioned to people on earth are often too the result of chance and accident and the way in which the material universe has been created and in which everything material works. May we do what lies in our power to prevent the accidents and miseries of earthly existence and to help the victims.

People: Father in heaven, grant us the will and wisdom to help effectively.

Priest: When we reflect on all the suffering in the world and all the things wrong with our society, we can easily be overcome with a sense of personal helplessness. Let us then throw ourselves on the Love of God and trust in him to ensure that in the end all will be well.

People: Father in heaven, grant us Grace and courage to change what should be changed, serenity to accept what cannot be changed, and wisdom to distinguish between the two.

Part 6—The Sacrament

Priest: Let us remember with gratitude the Passion of our friend and master, Jesus Christ: how his living revelation of God aroused in evil people the determination to destroy him, how he remained true to Love and let them kill him of their own free will, how he rose again and was for a short while seen on earth and then no more, how he sent the Holy Spirit at Pentecost, and how through these events his Mystical Body of all who believe in him was born on earth.

People: We remember.

Priest: Let us take this bread and wine and reenact the scene as Christ commanded us to do as a memorial to him. While Jesus was at table during his last meal with his disciples, he took the bread, broke it, and gave it to them saying, "Take it and eat; this is my body." Then he took the cup and said, "Drink all of you from this, for this is my blood, the blood of the promise, which is to be poured out for many for the forgiveness of sins." So I say to you *(holding up the bread/wafers)* "Look, this is the body of Christ!"

People: Look, the Body of Christ!

Priest: *(holding up the cup)* And this is the blood of Christ: the symbol of life and of God's promises to the human race!

People: Look, the blood of Christ!

Priest: As we eat this bread and drink this wine let us remember Christ's promise to dwell in all who believe in him and to open himself to let them dwell in him.

People: Jesus, dear friend and master, may we absorb your personality and become at one with you in your Mystical Body of all believers. By our entering into your divinity and your humanity, we want you to become fully ours and ourselves to become fully yours.

(People file up to the altar to receive the bread and wine. As he distributes the bread and wine, priest says to each communicant, "The body of Christ" and "The blood of Christ.")

Part 7—Thanksgiving and Resolution

Priest: Having feasted spiritually on the personality of our friend and master, the resurrected Christ, let us now rededicate ourselves to him. Let us remember with gratitude how, through his Son's Passion, God created the greatest good that he could do through the birth of Christ's Mystical Body out of the greatest evil people could perpetrate in the murder of his Son. He thus showed us how indeed God does create.

People: Father in heaven, in gratitude and Love we want to create as you create and thus to share in the Passion of your Son. Grant us through the power of your Grace to use every contact with misery or evil as an opportunity to spread Love and create new relationships of Love centered on you. Whatever misfortune life may bring to us, may we, like Jesus on the cross, remain true to Love.

Priest: May you indeed be true to the Love of God and thus to God himself. May the Grace of God and the personality of his Son shine through your life. As instruments in Christ's hands, may you infect others with Love and Faith and by your example bring them into the fellowship of Christ's Mystical Body. May the blessing of Father, Son, and Holy Spirit be upon you as you go out into the world and remain with you forever more.

People: In the name of Christ we go. We seek the joy of fulfilling ourselves in him.

(If hymns are inserted in some or all of the gaps between the parts of this form of service, they should be carefully selected or edited to ensure that what is sung does not conflict with what is said. The collection can best be taken at the end of part 5.)